BUT GOD...

IMPERFECT PEOPLE BEING SHAPED INTO HIS HANDS

JAMIE CHARLES

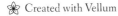

DEDICATION

This book is dedicated to the memory of three beautiful women who have touched my life and the life of our ministry. All three are waiting for us in Glory and I look forward to seeing them again at His throne.

Karen at her 60th birthday party in 2013 (photo courtesy of Joan Dawson)

Karen Kangas was the closest thing I've ever had to a sister. She was not only a dear friend but also the mother of my son-in-law, Davin. We shared many holiday dinners together, shared three precious grandchildren, and shared a common bond in our love for Jesus Christ. Karen made it very clear early on in our ministry that she would never be one to join us on a trip, but she wanted to be our support system at home. So when our children were too young to stay alone she volunteered to stay with them when we traveled. She even volunteered to stay with my elderly mother and care for her when we needed that help. She prayed for us, she sponsored children in our ministry, volunteered to help with some of our paperwork, and sustained us with her constant optimistic outlook on life. Even when she received her cancer diagnosis she remained positive until it became clear that her death was inevitable. And even after our children divorced, she remained that positive, loving influence in all our lives. Our children may have gone their separate ways but Karen never left any of us until God called her home on July 18, 2018.

Paula (wearing a purple dress) with her mother, LuAnn, and daughter, Heather, in Haiti in 2010

Paula Glenn had a powerful impact on my life even though we only met in person one time – on a trip to Haiti in October of 2010. She was the sort of person you would instantly choose to be your best friend. Paula's positive attitude and teachable spirit were a joy to experience on our trip and her willing attitude continued even after returning to the U.S. She volunteered to help us with some of our paperwork and even created documents for us. She wanted to go on another trip with us, but just a year and a half after that trip to Haiti she was diagnosed with cancer. She battled transparently – sharing with those of us who loved her about the battle taking place in her mind and in her heart. She never doubted God or His goodness and never gave up praising Him no matter how hard the battle became. When she lost all her hair during chemo she had a henna tattoo done on her sweet bald head with a scripture reference written on the side of her head right above her ear. When other patients were sitting next to her having their treatments they could see that scripture reference and would ask about it, allowing her to tell them about "Paula's Jesus."

That scripture was Job 42:5 NIV, *"My ears had heard of you, but now my eyes have seen you."*

Paula went to be with her Jesus on September 19, 2014, and now she is living that truth. Her ears heard about Him, she believed and served Him well, and now her eyes are seeing Him – face-to-face.

Bea with some Filipino friends in the Philippines in 2011

Bea Otte had an incredible heart for missions. After

her three children were grown, she went with a team that smuggled Bibles into China. She visited persecuted Christians in restricted areas in Asia, and went to Haiti and the Philippines with our ministry. Her love for orphans led her to adopt her fourth child from China as a single woman in her fifties. She had a heart for those with special needs acting as legal guardian for her younger brother with special needs. She was also a dear friend and neighbor since we lived very close to one another when God began His Hands Support Ministries. So it was an easy decision to ask Bea to serve on our board of directors - a position she gladly accepted - as one of the first seven board members of the ministry. We appreciated her heart to serve and her conservative perspective, often providing precisely the voice of reason we needed to hear at board meetings. It was a joy for our family to help her with her adopted son when he first came home from China. As a single mother, Bea had to work to provide for herself and her son, and we were honored to help care for him while she worked in a nursing home those first few years after he came to the U.S. It was a terrible shock to learn that she had been diagnosed with cancer in May of 2018, and less than a week later, on May 25, 2018, she left this life and entered the presence of her Lord and Savior, Jesus Christ. I have no doubt that she was greeted with those words we all long to hear – "Well done, my good and faithful servant."

ACKNOWLEDGMENTS

It takes a village to write a book. I have to start by thanking the Holy Spirit for continuing to nudge me until I finally responded in obedience and began to put words on the page. I have to thank my Father God for giving me the words to write. I also have to thank my Lord and Savior, Jesus Christ, for sacrificing himself for me so I could live for him and experience the amazing things I share with you in this book.

The list of people who have poured into this project to help bring it to completion is a long one. My fear in trying to list them is that I may overlook someone, so I will not mention specific names. You all know who you are.

I need to thank my friends and coworkers in the ministry for reminding me of stories to share and filling in some of the gaps in my memory. I need to thank the multitude of author friends who have given me wise counsel, helping me to see which path was the best one for me to take with this project. I need to thank those who have helped edit and polish this work to make it more enjoyable for you to read. I also need to thank my launch team for their willingness to help get this book into the hands of those God would have read it.

Most of all, I need to thank my husband, Philip, for being my sounding board and my support. I thank God every day for the gift of your life. Next time, it's my turn.

FOREWORD

HENRY COOPER

After 15 years serving as missionaries in Bolivia, S.A., my family and I returned to our home state of Maine and accepted a pastoral position at Fayette Baptist Church. In the summer of 2006, we made plans for the church's first short term mission trip – a team of 10 helping to build a church in northern Haiti with His Hands Support Ministries. Jamie, and her husband Philip, led the team.

Over the years, several from our church have taken trips with His Hands, have sponsored dozens of children, and financially supported the ministry. I am privileged to have a place on the His Hands board of directors. Through time and experience, I have gotten to know Jamie pretty well, but only in recent years (and now through this book) have I finally gotten to see her heart!

Jamie's philosophy of ministry is not something she would frame and hang on a wall. It is the way she and Philip live: Walk by faith, trust God, pray hard, put others first, serve out of a heart of compassion, give generously, and give God all the glory!

Jamie says,

> *God chooses the most unlikely people to accomplish*
> *His purposes. I would be very near the top of a list of*
> *unlikely choices.*

She is well aware that she is a flawed human being, but deeply believes that God uses broken vessels (cracked clay pots) who are fully devoted to Him, walking in obedience to what only He can do through them.

I agree with her children that Jamie is a true storyteller; sharing the many adventures she has experienced with precious people worldwide. Each story draws you in and makes you feel like you're right there on the journey with her. I found myself laughing out loud at the many humorous encounters, rejoicing with her to see God perform a miracle in someone's life, and even shedding a few tears as I looked through Jamie's eyes at the suffering that so many must endure in this world.

The stories in **But God...** are totally "Jamie" (no one will accuse her of plagiarism)! But it isn't about Jamie. **But God...** is really God's story; it is about what He is doing in and through His Church - His people to meet the basic and educational needs of children and adults living under the weight of poverty and physical hardship. This is a story about redemption, restoration, and beautiful relationships between God's children around the world.

As Jamie says,

> *We know God is busy weaving an intricate tapestry.*
> *From our perspective at the backside of His tapestry*

> *it just looks like a mess of unrelated threads. But when He finally shows us the front side of His tapestry, we will be amazed to see how all the threads come together to make an incredibly beautiful picture. But God...*

This is a book of short stories filled with powerful principles that apply to any Christian's life and ministry. As a pastor and missionary, I marvel at things like the decision to give 100% of the donations to the partner-hosts, never solicit funds for administration, and own no buildings or facilities. Those are innovative and ministry-multiplying policies that are virtually unheard of in other mission agencies or non-profits!

I believe it must make God smile to watch His children lead a ministry that promotes the practice that those on a mission team are there to "serve the host" and that they are there to serve at the host's invitation.

To quote Jamie,

> *if any adjustments needed to be made those adjustments would need to be made by us since we were the guests.*

But God...gave me a gentle rebuke; am I walking by faith so that when God presents an opportunity we should say "yes" and need to have a very good reason to say "no?" I also needed the strong reminder that *being outside of God's will for our lives is the riskiest place we could ever be,* and that *God frequently challenges us to do uncomfortable* *things...our ultimate desire is to walk in a way that's pleasing to Him even if it causes us to be uncomfortable; because it's all for His glory and His fame, not ours."*

Grab a hot cup of tea, sit in your favorite chair and join Jamie on her many adventures. Be ready to be deeply moved by stories like "the do-over" story about Heather or "Lazarus and Prayer around the World," the story of Philip's fatal heart attack and how God miraculously raised him from the dead to continue serving alongside Jamie. You will visit many countries and cultures.

Don't worry if you don't speak the language, *"things like language barriers, distance, and time are immaterial. Our faith in Christ unites us with a bond stronger than any earthly connection."*

If **But God...**was put to music, I believe it would be the song by musician and song writer, Chris Tomlin, "Not to Us."

Not to us, but to YOUR name be the glory
   Not to us, but to YOUR name be the glory
   Our hearts unfold before YOUR throne
   The only place for those who know
   It's not for us, It's all for YOU[1]

I highly recommend **But God...**a book that will both challenge and inspire you to trust God to take a risk, to step out by faith, and watch what He accomplishes – all for His Glory!

Henry Cooper -
Associate Pastor, Biblical Counsellor, Certified Life Coach

INTRODUCTION

I have given birth to six children. All six births were without pain medication. But I would have to say all six of those births were easier than writing this book has been. For years people kept telling me I needed to write this book because I needed to share these stories, these insights, and this history, with the world. It has been hard to bring myself to do it because I have felt unequal to the task of putting the story of this ministry into words. Also, the last thing I want is for the reader to come away with the idea that this is about me. But after going through four years of accumulated personal traumas, including the sudden cardiac death and subsequent resurrection of my husband, the passing of my ninety-nine-year-old mother, and the isolation of Covid-19 (including being sick with it myself for two months), which forced us to halt all foreign travel, I heard the Holy Spirit whispering in my soul that *now* was the time to stop and write this book. So with fear and trembling, I am writing it.

In the same way I have nurtured and poured into my six children to bring them to maturity and independence, I have nurtured and poured into my seventh child – a child we named His Hands Support Ministries. And in the same way that I don't want my children's lives and accomplishments to be about me, I don't want any of the achievements of His Hands to be about me. Because it's not, it's all for the glory and the fame of our Lord, Jesus Christ.

In the same way that my children ultimately belong to Him, so does this ministry. I am simply the flawed human being he used to help give birth to it, nurture it, and help it to grow to fruition. In the same way that I don't know when my children's lives will come to an end or when my involvement in their lives might end, I also don't know these things about His Hands. And that's okay because the outcome is not up to me. My job is simply to walk in the good works God has prepared for me beforehand and trust Him for the outcome – even with this book.

My kids call me a storyteller. I guess that's probably true. So I've chosen to write this book as though we were sitting together on a comfy couch, sipping hot African tea, while I tell you these stories God has used to lead us and to teach us. My goal in writing is to hopefully show how God can use the most unlikely people to accomplish His purposes. As you will soon see, I was turned off by missions. I lived in a teeny, tiny town in rural Western Maine. I spent most of my days at home, homeschooling my six children. My world view consisted of what happened within the four walls of our home. I had very little interest in what was happening outside of those walls. I had never been outside the United States, never held a passport, and led a very sheltered existence. But God made what seemed to be a ridiculous choice by choosing me to help give birth to this one small piece of His work with His children. Now this homeschooling mom is investing her life in advocating for children around the world to attend school. But I submit that it's exactly this choice that makes the most sense because it is abundantly clear that these are His works and not ours. We could never do any of these things in our own feeble strength or with our own feeble abilities. This is His work, not mine, and any honor, glory, or recognition goes to Him.

"Therefore, since through God's mercy we have this ministry, we do not lose heart...But we have this treasure in jars of clay to show that this all-surpassing power is from God and not from us." (2 Corinthians 4:1,7 New International Version)

"Not to us, Lord, not to us but to your name be the glory, because of your love and faithfulness." (*Psalm 115:1*)

My two oldest children, Kirstin (left) and Holly (right), with me in Haiti in 2012

My two middle children, Bethany (left) and Jacob (right) in Haiti in 2004

My youngest son, Sam with some young friends in the Democratic Republic of the Congo in 2009

My youngest daughter, Carolyn, with a little friend in Guatemala in 2014

I

OUR HISTORY

BACKGROUND

I hated missions. As awful as it is to admit, it's true – especially when you consider the fact that my father-in-law was a missionary in Lima, Peru, for three years when my husband, Philip, was a young boy. I had no interest in hearing about their stories or looking at the Peruvian artifacts they had brought home with them. No, I couldn't stand looking at those things. When missionaries would come to our church to give their slideshow reports, I would volunteer to sit in the nursery so I wouldn't have to be bored out of my mind. I had a dear friend, Pam Brochu, who was involved in mission trips to the country of Haiti. I thought she was nuts. No way would I ever do something like that. I mean, who in their right mind would want to?

However, our seventeen-year-old daughter, Holly, wanted to go on a mission trip to Haiti with a team from Faith Evangelical Free Church in Waterville, Maine, led by my friend Pam. I thought she had lost her mind. One of her friends had gone to Haiti with Pam and had visited a children's home there. When Holly heard her friend's report, she was sold. She wanted to volunteer at this children's home for a month! I rained a bit on her parade and told her she should probably consider going on a short trip first – to see if she could handle it – before she went and did anything crazy like volunteer at a children's home in Haiti for a month. We talked to Pam and let her know Holly was interested in going the next time, on the team led by Pam and a man from Faith Evangelical named Allan Stanford. Philip and I were not comfortable sending Holly to Haiti on her own – even if she would be going with Pam. So Philip did the unthinkable – he suggested I go with Holly. Holly's insanity must have been hereditary. Then the adventure of the idea grabbed hold, and I thought, *Why not?*

I had never been outside the United States before, except to Quebec Province in Canada. We lived in Maine at the time, so Canada hardly seemed like a foreign country to us. We lived a mere forty-five miles from the border, and, at that time, you didn't even need a passport to make the crossing. I had never even had a passport before. Despite this, we began to make plans for Holly and me to go to Haiti on the next trip, scheduled for January of 2002. In the summer of 2001, Pastor Apollon Noël, the Haitian minister with whom Pam's team would be working, visited Pam's home in Maine. All of the potential team members were invited to a gathering to meet Pastor Noël and talk with him about what a team might do for him if they came to visit his church in Haiti. He told us he was in the process of enlarging his church building, and only half of the roof was covered at that time. He needed a team to raise the needed financial support and then come down to Haiti and work with a Haitian work crew to put on the other half of the building's roof. Everyone thought that sounded great.

Then it hit me: Philip's profession is carpentry. He had

been a carpenter and done construction work for most of his adult life. It didn't make sense for *me* to accompany Holly on her trip to Haiti. They didn't need me – a homeschooling mom of six kids. They needed Philip – a carpenter by trade and the son of a pastor/missionary. After the gathering ended, I talked with Philip and told him it would be much more practical for him to go in my place. Then he said something that was one of the craziest things I had ever heard him say.

"No. If I go to Haiti, then all three of us are going."

I had absolutely no idea where we would get the money to pay for the three of us to go to Haiti. There was no way we could come up with that much money. I had no idea where we would get the money for two of us to go – never mind three! However, Philip was determined, so we moved forward with his plan. Before we could even get our passport applications, Holly's boyfriend, Davin, said he also wanted to go. In the end, in January of 2002, when I was 43 years old, Philip, Holly, Davin, and I went to Haiti with ten other people. For Philip and me, the world was never the same. (I still have no idea how we were ever able to pay for it. But God...)

To say our first trip to Haiti was an adventure would be an understatement. Right from the start, our first flight was delayed, so we missed our connection and every other connection after that. We spent a very short night in a hotel in a city we weren't even supposed to go to and landed in Haiti later than we had initially planned, and completely worn out from our journey. Davin was green due to airsickness from the *six* flights it took to get us there. The whole team loaded into an old school bus and started the ride from the city of Cap-Haitian out to the smaller city of Terrier Rouge, which is halfway between Cap-Haitian and the border of the Dominican Republic. The road had not been paved or maintained very well in those days, so the thirty-kilometer drive took two hours!

Since we arrived later than planned, it began to get dark on the long ride over the ridiculously bumpy dirt road. At that time, most of Haiti's Northeast Department did not have electricity. Once it got dark, it was completely black! We couldn't see anything along the roads until we came into various towns. Even then, all we could see was the eerie glow of candles making their meager effort to light up the vendors' stalls beside the road. The exhaustion of the trip combined with the unfamiliar sounds and smells, a language I couldn't begin to understand, and then the creepy candlelight, stirred up a real spirit of fear in me. I began to panic and was silently calling out to God, asking Him why He had brought me here and asking him to bring me home by some miracle. If it had been possible to get on a plane right then and go home, I would have done it. No question. I was angry at myself for giving in to a spirit of adventure and making this trip to a place that seemed so foreign to me it might as well have been on another planet.

I sat in my seat and turned to look out the window, not because I thought I could see anything in the pitch-black darkness but because I didn't want anyone to see the tears running down my face. Then it happened. I looked up at the sky and saw the Big Dipper, and peace came over me. I realized the sky was the same, the stars were the same, and God was the same. He knew where I was and had His hand on me and had His purpose in me being on that bus. And then everything was okay.

That trip exposed me to a world I didn't know existed. I always thought life in the U.S. was real life and that life in developing countries was weird, strange, and uncommon.

That trip taught me that life in the U.S. is not real life. Life in the U.S. is what's weird, strange, and uncommon. The majority of the world does not experience that kind of life. What we consider to be Third World countries are really Majority World countries. The way life is in those countries is far more realistic than what we experience living in the U.S. I also learned that, even though their lives are very different from what we experience, our Haitian brothers and sisters were not all that different from us. We shared a palpable common bond in Jesus Christ. In the end, that's all that mattered. To say that first trip to Haiti wrecked me would be an understatement. That first trip to Haiti tore up my insides and turned me completely inside out, and changed my entire view of life and of missions. I have never been the same since and, for that, I am eternally grateful.

January 2002 Haiti team

2

SEEDS ARE PLANTED

Coming home from our first trip to Haiti was more of a culture shock than going to Haiti had been. I looked at everything completely differently. A trip to the grocery store brought back visions of children using their fingernails to scrape the burnt, stuck-on rice off the bottom of the huge cooking pot so they could have a little bit more food in their bellies: and the tears would start. A trip to Wal-Mart would make me think about buying shoes or school supplies for Solondjie or one of the other sweet children we had met: and the tears would start. During evening service at church, I would glance across the room and make eye contact with Holly, and we would both start to cry for reasons we couldn't express. I was wrecked, and the person I was pre-Haiti didn't exist anymore. I was left as a shattered person who knew God had a specific plan for us in Haiti, but I had no idea what it might be.

Philip and I were impacted so strongly that we knew we couldn't put our photos in an album and put them on a shelf to be forgotten. We couldn't check off "mission trip to Haiti" on some imaginary bucket list. We both knew God had something for us, but we didn't know what, and it left us feeling shaken to the point where we wondered if we had somehow gotten sick. It was a feeling that was hard to pin down, but as time passed and God spoke to our hearts, we knew we had to talk to Pastor Noël.

In the summer of 2002, when Pastor Noël revisited Maine, we found ourselves sitting with him at Pam's dining room table, and we simply asked him what we could do. We told him we felt like God was pushing us to help him somehow in his ministry, but we had no idea how we could help. His answer was simple: find people who are willing to pay for children to go to school. There it was: our mandate. God wanted us to find people who would be willing to pay for Haitian children to attend the school that was part of Pastor Noël's church in Terrier Rouge.

As we prepared to return to Haiti with the team going from New Hope Evangelical Free Church in Solon, Maine (a daughter church of Faith Evangelical) in January of 2003, we knew one of the things we would be doing on that trip was to get names of children who needed help. We had no idea how we would do that, but it didn't matter. We would figure it out with God's help. Once we arrived in Haiti and Pastor Noël handed us a list of names – the names of fifty-seven children who needed a sponsor in January of 2003 – we had no idea how we would go about finding those sponsors. Our hometown in Maine was very remote with only 600 people, and we attended a church that had less than fifty-seven people in it. Most of my days were spent at home with my children, who were ages seven to twenty at that time, without a car, and with little access to large groups of people. I had no idea how we could do this – but God did.

Once we returned home, the biggest stumbling block

was that we only had a list of names and nothing else. We had to ask one of our Haitian friends to tell us which names were girls' names and which were boys' names. We didn't know what age, grade, or any family information on the children. We also had no photos of them. Eventually, we had seven brave souls willing to sponsor a name on a scrap of paper without any other information. We knew if we were going to find sponsors for the rest of the children, we would have to go back to Haiti and get more information.

One Sunday evening, Pam and I were given a few minutes to speak to her church about the opportunity to sponsor a child in Haiti. After that service, Philip and I took Pam aside and asked her when Faith Evangelical would be scheduling the next trip to Haiti. She told us trips didn't necessarily happen every year, so she didn't know if there would even be a trip in 2004. At that moment, Philip turned to me and said the second-craziest thing he had ever said to me.

"Well, then we'll just have to put together a trip on our own and go."

So how do we do this?? How do we put together our own team, plan the logistics for that team, and then do what we need to do when we get to Haiti? These were overwhelming questions to me at that time in my sheltered life. We started asking the questions one at a time and broke things down step by step. Eventually, we had a plan for five of us to head back to Haiti in June of 2003. With us on that trip were our oldest daughter, Kirstin, her friend from Word of Life Bible Institute, Rachel, and another dear friend, Tiffany, who is a professional photographer. The five of us headed back to Haiti, determined to figure out how to do this thing that God had asked us to do.

Our family had been involved in sponsoring children in

another organization since 1986, so we at least had an idea of the kind of information a sponsor might want to have. Despite this, I really had no idea what questions we should ask or how to ask them since I didn't yet speak Haitian Creole. I didn't need to worry about all that because Pastor Noël had a plan. He had us work with his secretary for the school, who spoke English, and knew most of the children personally. She was able to answer the feeble questions I had come up with. The idea of creating an interview form to use had never occurred to me, so I had a spiral notebook on my lap and simply scribbled down the names and the information as the secretary gave them to me. In hindsight, I realized some of the questions I asked should have been asked differently. I also should have asked follow up questions for clarification, but somehow it all worked out, and we ended up with basic information on each child on that list of fifty-seven children, along with several more children Pastor Noël added during our visit.

Kirstin and Rachel figured out the best way to measure the children's height and weight. They traced the children's feet so we could figure out a shoe size later. Tiffany used her photography skills to take beautiful photos of the children. In that way, the foundation was laid for every trip we have done since then. We've refined the process many times and will probably continue to refine it as time passes, but that first information-gathering trip set the stage for everything that came after it, and it was good.

Having Philip and I lead the team gave us a completely different dynamic on the vital aspect of building up the relationships God had brought into our lives with our partners and the children. At times we struggled with language and cultural differences, but we got past those by focusing on our common bond of faith in Jesus Christ and our mutual love and respect for one another. We realized we had a lot to learn from our new friends, and if any adjustments were needed those adjustments would need to be made by us since we were the guests.

Since we're talking about Haiti, we can't overlook the very real presence of voodoo and spirit worship–something that can impact me spiritually. Because of negative influences when I was young, occultic practices are something to which I am particularly sensitive and try to avoid, but it's difficult to do that in a place like Haiti. On the first night of our previous trip in January of 2003, I was lying in bed trying to sleep. The sound of the voodoo drums in the distance began to unnerve me, and I felt the fear rising. The louder the drums got, the worse the fear became until I was paralyzed with fear. I felt the presence of evil just above my face as I lay in my bed, which I now recognize as spiritual oppression. I literally could not move. In my mind, I was crying out to God to save me and take me back home but was still unable to move. The more I prayed and cried out in my mind, the evil presence left me, and I was finally able to reach under my pillow for my flashlight and turn it on. The presence of the light drove away the fear, and I was able to finally rest in faith that God knew where I was and had His hand over me. Looking back, I have wondered if that was some kind of test of the enemy to see if he could keep me from walking in the good works God had prepared for me. If it was, the enemy failed.

On this first trip led by Philip and me, we had another experience with an evil presence in a different manifestation. One of the things we enjoyed doing as a team was simply walking around the community, taking in the sights, sounds, and smells, and trying to learn more about the beautiful Haitian culture. We always walked with a Haitian chaperone to help us navigate our way.

While we were walking one day, a man was walking towards us on the opposite side of the street. He was obviously under the influence of something, so we were trying to keep our distance. Our chaperone indicated to us that this man used drugs and drank alcohol, so we assumed he was under those kinds of influences that day. We also knew he practiced voodoo since he was someone Philip and I, but not the rest of the team, had met previously. Our Haitian friends always referred to Rachel in the French form – Rachelle – so it was beyond startling when this man saw us, crossed the street, came directly towards us, and raised his finger pointing it at Rachel. He called out in a very deep and loud voice, *"Rachel!!!"* Not Rachelle – but Rachel. We have no idea how he knew her name or why he would say it in the English version and not the French form like our Haitian friends did. The hair on the back of our necks stood straight up. We turned and walked away as quickly as possible. Again, I believe the enemy was challenging us to see if he could keep us from accomplishing the good works God had for us. Again, he failed.

When we returned to Maine at the end of that trip, we received an invitation to give a short presentation at Faith Evangelical on this brand-new sponsorship program. At the end of that day, we had run out of children who needed a sponsor and had started a waiting list of people who wanted to sponsor a child once we had information on additional children. I had looked at that list of fifty-seven children, got completely overwhelmed, and thought there was no way I could ever find sponsors for all of those kids. I was right – I couldn't, but God...

Children of Haiti

3

BIRTH OF A MINISTRY

W e never intended to start a ministry. We didn't wake up one morning and say, "Hey! I've got a great idea! Let's start a ministry!" No, that was all God's plan. We believe it is perfectly illustrated in the verse we have chosen as our touchstone for this ministry we never intended to start. Ephesians 2:10 NKJV says, "For we are His workmanship, created in Christ Jesus for good works, which God prepared beforehand, that we should walk in them."

That's all we've been trying to do since those first seeds were planted back in 2002. We simply want to walk in the good works God has already prepared for us.

That hasn't always been as simple as it sounds, though. Initially, we had people who wanted to give us donations, so we knew we should open a bank account. When I naïvely walked into the bank in 2003 and asked to open an account in the name of a non-established organization, I got an education I didn't know I needed. I was instructed to contact the IRS and first get an EIN. (I didn't even know what an EIN was at that time!) Then I could come back to the bank and open an account using that EIN.

Contacting the IRS was frightening but more helpful than I anticipated. I discovered that as long as we didn't have more than $10,000 passing through our account in a single year, there was nothing else we needed to do.[1] Great! In order to apply for an EIN, we needed a name for our non-established organization. We decided to come up with a great name in Haitian Creole and used it when we filled out the EIN application. We sent in our application and received approval in the mail, and I went back to the bank to open our first account. We learned later that, not only did I use the wrong grammatical structure for the name, it also proved to be difficult for people to pronounce or to spell. We ran with it anyway, since we already had the EIN, and then spent the next four years spending way too much time telling people how to say it, how to spell it, and what it meant.

Since we were not recognized as a 501(c)3 organization at that time, we could not give out tax receipts. Sponsorship checks were made out directly to Pastor Noël, and we simply gathered them all up and mailed them to him in batches. This proved problematic when checks were either made out incorrectly or bounced, causing problems for Pastor Noël and us.

Then we had someone ask to make a sizable donation for our general use, but they also needed a tax receipt. The only way we could do this was to become an official ministry of our local church, First Baptist Church of Kingfield, Maine. The check could be made out to the church, a tax receipt given to the donor, and then the money transferred over to our organization's bank account. This worked for a while, but then we found ourselves in an uncomfortable position at congregational meetings when we would see the church's treasurer's report. The funds passing through for our ministry were more than what the church received in their general fund for that quarter.

We had a friend contact us asking if we would like her to set up a website for us. We agreed, realizing this would be another way we could spread the word and bring in new sponsors. Once she had the website set up, we began having people from outside the U.S. come across our website and decide to sponsor a child using PayPal to make their sponsorship donations. This increased the amount of money coming into the ministry's bank account. As a result, we began to surpass that limit of $10,000 per year going through our account. Then God started to reveal His greater plan to us to extend our reach outside the country of Haiti. It was then we realized we were going to have to grow up and do things like a real organization and file for tax-exempt status. We had no idea how to do that.

In early 2007, when Philip was doing construction work for a lawyer, he asked him if we could meet with him to find out what we needed to do. We learned we first had to form a corporation. Then the corporation would apply for tax-exempt status. Again, we had no idea how to do any of that. The lawyer walked us through the process of incorporating, with us randomly nominating officers from among the names of people involved in the ministry who had said they would serve on a board of directors.

We also used this opportunity to change the ministry's name to one that was easier for people to spell and pronounce. It also acknowledged that God had plans to expand us beyond the country of Haiti when the name His

Hands Support Ministries was chosen. Once our corporation was established in the state of Maine, we had to file for tax-exempt status. By doing a Google search, we found a company online that specialized in this process, and we hired them.

At the end of 2007, we received our approval letter from the IRS, making His Hands Support Ministries an officially recognized tax-exempt organization. This was something we had never planned to do and never really intended to do. But God obviously had other plans. There were a lot of things we didn't know how to do and never really wanted to know how to do: things like how to work on a website or how to use accounting software. But God was with us and directed us to people who could help, and somehow He created a functioning ministry. Even today, if you were to ask Philip or me if we are the founders of the ministry, our answer is likely to go something like this, "No, we are simply the flawed human beings God used to start it."

Why did we choose the name His Hands Support Ministries? We certainly considered shorter options. However, nothing else we came up with seemed to fit with the key elements important to us: to promote unity in the body of Christ and to support and encourage our brothers and sisters in Christ in poverty around the world.

For years our tiny little home church of First Baptist focused on studying the importance of promoting unity in the body of Christ. It's something we have tried to promote on a personal level in our own small ways. We would often visit other churches in our area just to get to know the believers who chose to fellowship there, trying to break down some of the denominational barriers that only serve to divide those who all share the common bond of faith in Jesus Christ and have experienced His saving grace.

When God began to take us to Haiti (and then to other parts of the world) to spend time with our brothers and sisters overseas, we simply saw that as an extension of what we had already been doing in trying to promote unity in the body of Christ. Our purpose in establishing these relationships with other believers overseas was never to start our own American work in another country. It was to come alongside our brothers and sisters to support and encourage them in the work they were already doing. In Exodus 17:10-13 NIV we read,

> "So Joshua fought the Amalekites as Moses had ordered, and Moses, Aaron, and Hur went to the top of the hill. As long as Moses held up his hands, the Israelites were winning, but whenever he lowered his hands, the Amalekites were winning. When Moses' hands grew tired, they took a stone and put it under him, and he sat on it. Aaron and Hur held his hands up—one on one side, one on the other—so that his hands remained steady till sunset. So Joshua overcame the Amalekite army with the sword."

In this story, our ministry partners would be filling the role of Moses, and His Hands Support Ministries would be filling the role of Aaron and Hur. We want to come alongside our ministry partners and help hold up their arms – to support them in the battles they fight in trying to provide for their own people's needs, both physical and spiritual.

In observing how Pastor Noël fought his battles, it was evident that he was a man who had learned to do everything by faith. Many times we had heard him say, "If God gives me one dollar, I will work with one. If he gives me two dollars, I will work with two." He also told us this story – it was the end of the school term, and the time had come to pay the teachers. However, he didn't have the money he needed to pay them, so he went to a friend and asked to borrow the money. His friend loaned it to him, and Pastor Noël went on his way. Along the way, he went to the post office to get his mail, where he received an unexpected letter from a friend. In it was a check for the exact amount he had just borrowed. Instead of rejoicing at God's unexpected provision, he said he had to stop and pray and repent of his unbelief. Instead of believing God and trusting Him to provide, he had gone to a friend and borrowed the money. Hearing stories like that and watching how he would step out in faith with every facet of his ministry, we knew we needed to model that incredible example and operate our ministry in the same way, by faith.

As a result, it became our practice never to solicit support for our administrative costs, which have increased exponentially with the ministry's growth. When asked to speak, we will share the needs of our partners, but we do not ask for support for our administrative costs: and God has been faithful.

Unlike many other ministries similar to ours, we are not a ministry that shows up in another country with money to hand out. We come to gather information, pray, encourage our partners and the children's families to pray as well, and then watch how God provides. We've often joked that we should have named the ministry Conduit Ministries since the money comes in one side and then just flows out the other.

We also made the decision to run this ministry entirely with volunteers so there would be no overhead costs for salaries: again, trusting God to meet our needs in this area. Our choice to operate in this way means we can send one hundred percent of all designated donations to our partners. None of it gets used for our operational expenses.

We also made the decision to own as little as possible. We have no office building or any other property, we don't own any vehicles, and we own very little equipment. This means we are not in a position where we are forced to raise funds to "feed the beast," so to speak, and it frees us up to be able to do more with the small amount of undesignated funds we receive.

Not owning a building means there is no centralized location where our work has to take place. This means we can have volunteers in key positions that are able to work from their own homes all across the country. This would not have been possible before the internet, but now, with online file sharing, our volunteers can live anywhere. Our current program coordinators are living in Maine, New Hampshire, Massachusetts, Virginia, Georgia, Florida, Oregon, and California. One volunteer is currently living in the country of Mexico. Each one is equipped to do what they need to do right there in their own home.

All volunteer also means we are frugal. Many times it means we end up sleeping in an airport rather than spending money on an expensive hotel room. Sometimes it means we stay in places that may make us uncomfortable: like a mission compound in Rwanda where the legs of my bed literally snapped halfway through the night, and I thought I might roll into the bathroom where I was afraid a mamba might come up out of the toilet. Then there have been other times where God blessed us with incredibly beautiful and comfortable places to stay: like the private resort villa in Bali with our own private pool we got to share with twenty children from an orphanage we invited to come visit us. We felt guilty about being blessed with such luxurious accommodations, but the guilt was replaced with thankfulness when we were able to share it with them. In every case, God has been faithful.

As the ministry has grown, we have found ourselves in painful situations at times: something our dear sister in Christ and board member, Bea, used to describe as growing pains. Since the beginning, we have been figuring things out as we go along. We never had another ministry that was further down the road of good works that could point out the way for us to follow or explain how things should be done. In hindsight, I see this as a good thing because we could only rely on direction from God and not the wisdom of men. I believe that's the only way this ministry has experienced any growth and had any kind of positive influence in the lives of those who have been touched by it.

As growth has occurred, we have needed to suggest much-needed changes in the process. At times those suggestions have been misconstrued or misunderstood, causing more growing pains, but ultimately our desire to walk in the good works God has prepared for us beforehand directed us in the ways He would have us go whether or not they were pleasing on a personal level. Just like any other ministry, we have had difficult people become involved. Dealing with the issues they created caused growing pains, caused us to carefully examine what we were doing and how we were doing it and forced us to grow as a ministry.

Even in these difficulties, we see blessings and praise God for growing us more through it. In the end, this is His ministry, not ours, and our ultimate desire is to walk in a way that's pleasing to Him even if it causes us to be uncomfortable; because it's all for His glory and His fame, not ours.

This photo is from our first trip to Haiti in 2002. The hands in the photo belong to Philip and one of the Haitian workmen who worked on the church roof project with our team. He agreed to pose for this photo in exchange for having us come to his house and take photos of his family, which we did. It has become the photo we use to represent our ministry but we had no idea about any of this when the photo was taken. But God...

4

BRANCHING OUT

S ometimes I question my sanity. At times thoughts pop into my head, and they can't be traced back to where they started. I suppose instead of thinking I might be crazy, maybe, just maybe, those thoughts were put there by the Holy Spirit, and it's up to me to figure out why. Rwanda was one of those thoughts. After we had established our ministry in Haiti, had figured out how to find sponsors for children and provide information to those sponsors, began to feel comfortable with the role God had given us, and gained some experience doing what He had for us to do, the thought of duplicating in Rwanda what we were already doing in Haiti popped into my mind. Why Rwanda? I have no idea. That's the crazy part.

I didn't know much about Rwanda at the time. I had heard little bits of information about a terrible genocide some years earlier, but that's about all I knew. I didn't know anyone there, nor did I have any contacts there. There was no way to take our formula and get it rolling in Rwanda. The thought was so crazy I didn't even share it with Philip for a while. However, eventually, the thought came out. I don't remember where or how. To his credit, he didn't think it was crazy and was open to the idea. There we both were, with a heart to help children in Rwanda but no way to bring it to fruition.

One evening we were watching a television program about a well-known ministry that worked with pastors in Rwanda. I thought contacting them would be the perfect way to get in touch with someone in Rwanda who could use the type of help we could provide. I sent an email to that well-known ministry, explaining who we were and how God was using us. I asked them if they knew any pastors in Rwanda who needed the type of help we could provide and then gave them a link to our website to validate what I had just told them. Then I waited for the anticipated response… which never came. I tried again. Resent the message and waited for a response… which never came. It was extremely difficult for both Philip and me to put that dream on the back burner, but we felt we had no choice. We had no way of making it happen, so we just shelved the idea without sharing it with anyone else.

Fast forward to a time in 2006 when I was opening an email from a sponsor in the Haiti program. She had been searching online for a ministry in Africa called Shalom Ministries and came across a ministry by that name and made contact with the pastor. They communicated for a while, and then he told her he was interested in setting up a sponsorship program. In her email, she asked if we would be interested. Would we be interested?! I was bouncing up and down in my desk chair, yelling over to Philip that we had a possible contact in Africa! This sponsor had absolutely no idea God had been putting Rwanda on our hearts, and there she was, asking us if we would be interested in helping a pastor in Africa! Ever the more stable one, Philip told me to calm down and ask her where in Africa the pastor was located. He reminded me, "Africa's a big place." I tried to settle myself down and wrote back to the sponsor, very nonchalantly saying, "We might be interested. Where is the pastor located?" Well, you may have heard my reaction when she wrote back because I literally screamed when she answered me saying, "Uganda, *Rwanda*, and the Congo."

This was *it*! The dream we had hoped and prayed for and God had put it right in our path; right in our lap! (What we didn't know at the time, and what makes this connection even more God-ordained, is the fact that the Shalom Ministries the sponsor had found was not the one she had been seeking. She had made a mistake in the initial connection but continued in their communications even after she discovered it was not the ministry she actually sought.) We initiated communication with this pastor, who was living in Uganda, through the sponsor at first and then directly, later on, asking some initial questions to find out if our model would even work in his ministry. We were thrilled to discover it would.

Then the enemy crept in and planted seeds of doubt. We started questioning ourselves, questioning our motives. How could we agree to go to Africa and meet this pastor when going there was *our* dream, *our* plan? We had this crazy idea if God wanted us to do something, it would probably be something we didn't want to do. How could He ask us to do something we already dreamed of doing? We were afraid to say yes because we were afraid we were only saying yes because it was what *we* wanted and not what *God* wanted.

As I prayed about it, I was begging God for a literal neon sign because I did not want to make the trip to Africa without very clear, plain direction from Him that it was, indeed, what He wanted.

During this difficult season of praying for a neon sign, I had a friend named Terry who was making a trip to Haiti to work with Pastor Noël in early January of 2007. She didn't have anyone to go with her, so I volunteered to go along. We flew out of Portland, Maine, just a few days after New Year's Day. The flights were all very full, and the security line was long, so by the time we got to our gate, they had closed our flight. We had already checked in, our suitcases were on the plane, but the gate agent had already given away our seats and refused to reopen the cabin door and let us board.

I stood there at the desk at the gate, calmly but firmly asking her what she was going to do for us because she should never have given our seats away. She said there were no more flights from Portland that day but asked if we had a car at the airport so we could get to Boston. When I told her we had no car at the airport, she said the airline would give us a voucher for a cab to take us to Logan Airport in Boston where we could catch a flight. We would have to hurry because we didn't have a lot of time before our Boston flight would depart. She said she had already called a cab for us and it would be waiting at the curb when we got there, so we needed to go quickly.

We found the cab right where she told us it would be, and the driver greeted us and started putting our hand baggage in the trunk. As he was doing this, he was talking to us about where we needed to go and how quickly we needed to get there. It was impossible *not* to notice his strong, foreign accent and his dark-colored skin. When we got into the cab, Terry asked him where he was from, wondering if this driver the airline had ordered for us would be from Haiti. Imagine that providential sign! Instead, as he started frantically driving, he laughed and said, "Oh... I'm from Uganda!" When I heard that, and when I thought about all the possible cab drivers we could have gotten in Portland, Maine, and I realized this one was from *Uganda*, I started to laugh hysterically. Terry wondered what was so funny so I turned to her, laughed some more, and said, "You have no idea, but this cab is being driven by a neon sign!" When we landed in Miami and got to our hotel for the night before heading to Haiti the next morning, I called Philip and said, "We're going to Africa."

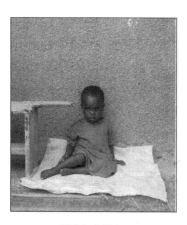

Child of Africa

5

WE GO TO AFRICA

How does one prepare for a trip to a country they've never visited before to meet someone they've never met before? Just asking that question makes it sound as crazy as it was. The first thing we did was prepare ourselves for a different culture with different practices and expectations. We also wanted to learn some of the histories of Uganda, Rwanda, and the Democratic Republic of the Congo. We did a lot of reading and a lot of online research. Then we watched three movies. Those movies scared me to death but not because of the violence, hardship, and poverty portrayed in them. They scared me because there was a running theme in all three. The theme was simple yet profound. It can be summed up in a statement that goes something like this, a statement that was echoed in each of the three movies – "Who do you Westerners think you are, coming over here with your cameras and your hand sanitizer and your plans?" That's not a direct quote from any of those movies, but it might as well be, and that's how I began to feel.

Who were we? We were two uninformed, rural

Mainers who had lots of zeal but not much experience. What did we think we would be able to do that Africans themselves couldn't do? I realize now this was the enemy trying to discourage us again and take our eyes off the path God had prepared for us. Who were we? We were children of the King who were simply walking in the good works He had put right in our path. The only way to avoid doing them would be to walk around them and get off the path He had prepared for us.

There we were the night before our departure for Entebbe, Uganda, in May of 2007, sending emails to the people we knew who had some type of contact with our potential new partner, asking them if they had any pictures of him. We realized we had no idea how we would know which dark-skinned African man would be the one we should be looking for when we arrived at the airport in Uganda, and we needed some physical assurance like a photo. We did receive one, and the next day we were on a flight to Entebbe, literally pinching one another, trying to convince ourselves this was real.

We didn't need to worry about how we would know who Pastor Stephen Bamuleke, better known as "Bamo," was when we arrived at the airport. The minute we saw each other, it was as if we had known each other forever. There was an instantaneous connection that can only come from our common bond in Jesus Christ. So all our fears and trepidations left us, and we simply sat back in the car, taking in the overwhelming sights, sounds, and smells of Uganda. We couldn't help but make comparisons to Haiti because they were very much alike in many ways. But there were also some big differences. English is the official language in Uganda, they drive on the other side of the road, and the women were dressed in long skirts fashioned from beautiful

African batiks. It was beautiful, but the similarities of seeing the same kinds of poverty that we faced in Haiti were heartbreaking. We knew God had His purposes in bringing us here when we saw the children desperate for help to gain access to education.

Our first Sunday in Uganda was an experience that's still hard to describe. We attended a church service in a slum of Kampala in a ramshackle church building, but the powerful praise and worship which flowed from that building were what I like to imagine heaven will be like. Pastor Bamo brought us up on the platform to introduce us to those who had gathered. He was at a loss for words when he tried to explain how we had met one another and ended up saying this, "I can't even explain to you how I met these people. It was a miracle from God." And he was right.

As we sat through that service, we remained in awe of how God had orchestrated all of this and had brought us together with an African man who was so like-minded it was like we all shared the same brain. Only God could do that. Then we received the incredible blessing of being treated to a traditional African celebratory dance that is beyond description. The colorful batiks, the grass skirts, men on stilts, the voices ululating.[1] It was a sensory overload of the most incredible kind, and all Philip and I could do was to sit there and smile, laugh, shake our heads, and pinch ourselves. Yes, we really were in Africa, and it was incredible.

On our first day of meeting and documenting children in Kampala, we met a little girl named Miracle. Her name was just another confirmation for us of what God had done in bringing us to Africa. Philip had his photo taken with Miracle and another little girl sitting on his lap, and he uses that photo as his profile photo on Facebook to this day. I like to think that not only was it confirmation that God had performed a miracle in bringing us to Africa and giving us the deepest desire of our hearts at that time, but it was also a foreshadowing of things to come.

After spending several days in Uganda visiting a few cities and towns and documenting children for the sponsorship program, we finally made the journey across Rwanda's border. This place had captured our hearts before we even knew much about it. One of Rwanda's most well-known facts is that the country experienced a horrible genocide that started in April of 1994.In one hundred days, close to one million people from the Tutsi tribe, along with people from the Hutu tribe who were considered moderates, were slaughtered. It boggles the mind to think about it. However, what we didn't know, or expect, before going there was the beauty of the country. Crossing the border into Rwanda was a very emotional experience for Philip and me.

When you cross a land border in Africa, you must pass through immigration in the country you are exiting first. Then you must walk across a boundary area, rather like a no man's land, before you cross the border into the country you are entering, where you must pass through immigration again. When we officially exited Uganda and then walked through the boundary area on foot, our emotions began to swell. We reached out to hold each other's hands and then stepped across the border into Rwanda together, at the same time. It's hard to explain the feeling we got once we were officially in Rwanda. It was a dream realized.

Yes, it says in Psalm 37:4 NKJV, "Delight yourself also in the Lord, and He shall give you the desires of your heart." However, I like to think this scripture's meaning is a bit different from what we think at first glance. I believe it means if we're following the Lord's leading, the desires we have in our hearts will be there because He put them there. We didn't need to make our decision to go to Rwanda so difficult. We were doing our best to walk in the good works God had prepared for us beforehand. Then a desire took root in our hearts. Then the opportunity to fulfill that desire presented itself. It lined up perfectly with what God had been calling us to do. It should have been an easy decision to make, and I regret turning it into such an unnecessary reason for inner conflict.

In Kigali, the capital of Rwanda, we were offered an opportunity to visit the Genocide Memorial: a museum of remembrance of the genocide as well as the final resting place of 250,000 people who lost their lives in the genocide. It was a hard thing to do, but we knew we needed to go there so we could understand what these people had experienced just thirteen short years before. Seeing the exhibits and reading about the history leading up to the genocide, and then about the genocide itself, was excruciating. It was so hard to imagine actually living through it. A Rwandan woman was walking through the museum just ahead of us on the directed path. It hurt my heart to watch her reading the information and looking at the displays, all the while with tears streaming down her face and her hand pounding her chest. Unimaginable.

When we were interviewing the children and their parents in Kigali, it was hard to forget all of these parents had lived through what happened there. For them, it was recent history. We sensed a profound sadness in Rwanda even though the genocide is not often discussed. It is now illegal in Rwanda to even speak about one's ethnicity, so it is not something anyone would discuss. But it was hard for Philip and me to get it out of our minds. When we drove through the streets, we thought about scenes from the movies we had watched, as many of them looked the same in real life as they did in the movies. Rwanda is a beautiful country with an unimaginable tragedy in its history.

After spending time in Rwanda, we didn't know what to expect in the Congo. Much of the hostilities of the genocide crossed the border into the Congo (then Zaire), and some of those hostilities continue to this day. It is, by far, the most devastated country we visit. There are levels of poverty that are unimaginable, intermixed with hostilities between tribes, between rebel forces and government forces, causing much suffering, especially among the children. As sad as Rwanda seemed under the surface, the sadness is inescapable in the Congo. It was a very difficult place for us to visit so early in our ministry. We thank God for bringing us to all three places, and we know, without a doubt, that He planted that desire in our hearts before He ever showed us how He would bring it to fruition. But God...

Philip and Miracle with another little friend

6

UNITY AND GUATEMALA

Now that we had made our long-desired trip to Africa, what was next? How and where was God going to direct us as we continued to walk in the good works He had prepared for us? At that time I felt like God had placed the country of Guatemala on my heart, but, again, it seemed crazy. I knew very little about Guatemala other than the fact that our dear friends had adopted their daughter from Guatemala twenty years earlier. It really didn't make sense to have Guatemala on my heart, and I didn't know what to do with that desire. I finally decided to confirm my foolish nature by trying to contact a woman with whom I had a mutual friend. This woman had a ministry in Guatemala, so I figured she would surely direct us to someone there who could use the kind of help we could provide. Plus, I felt more confident in approaching her because we shared a mutual friend who could confirm we were a legitimate ministry. I sent her an email introducing myself, dropping the name of our mutual friend, and asking her about providing a contact in Guatemala who could use the kind of help we could provide. I think you can guess what happened. Not. One. Thing. I never received a response to the multiple emails I sent her. I was left with no choice but to put that desire on the back burner and continue walking in the good works God had already put right in front of us.

One of those works continued to be promoting unity in the body of Christ. We remained close to our friend Pam who had brought us to Haiti in the first place. Pam continued working with her medical ministry, called Haitian Ministries,[1] putting her nursing skills to good use, while we continued working in cooperation with her, consulting her when we had questions about a child's medical needs and keeping one another up to date on things pertaining to Haiti within our ministry. We believe that building unity isn't just something we do with our international partners or within the confines of our own ministry, but we also feel it's important to strive for with other like-minded ministries.

Within this mindset, I was intrigued by some email communication, which began with a man named Mike Bell from the Salt Lake area of Utah in 2008. As one of his church's pastors, Mike had become concerned about the church's response to global poverty and asked himself who was our closest, poorest global neighbor. This led him to do a lot of online research on the country of Haiti, where he stumbled upon our ministry's website. We had some great email conversations, which led me to challenge him to go on a trip to Haiti with us. As a result, in October of 2008, Mike, his wife, Joani, and three others from their church, joined us on a trip to Haiti. This led to a long-standing relationship between His Hands and Mike and Joani, along with many others from their church, which continues to this day. It also led Mike to join a different ministry, addressing global poverty through church partnerships and eventually branching out and establishing his own ministry called Healing Nations.[2] His Hands still works in cooperation with Healing Nations and shares some common overseas ministry partners with them.

So in early 2009, I was not surprised to see an email in my inbox from Mike Bell. However, I was completely dumbfounded when I opened the email and read one of his first sentences. "Have you ever thought about doing His Hands for Guatemala?" Mike knew nothing about my heart's desire to reproduce in Guatemala what we were already doing in Haiti and East Africa. He was in Guatemala at the time, doing an investigative trip with the first international ministry he worked with, and they were interviewing potential new partners in Guatemala. One of those men, a pastor named Merari Rodrigues, was a perfect fit for our ministry.

As a result of this connection, in the late summer of 2009, we sent a team of eighteen – three from His Hands and fifteen from Eliot Baptist Church in Southern Maine - to visit Pastor Merari for the first time. This team laid the groundwork for a follow-up team in December of 2009 when the information was gathered on the first children to be put into the sponsorship program. All these teams have led to an incredible partnership not only between Pastor Merari and His Hands but also between Pastor Merari and Healing Nations and Eliot Baptist Church. We believe the ideal of creating unity in the body has been strengthened significantly with all these ministries working together. Also, due to the number of teams being sent by His Hands, Healing Nations, and Eliot Baptist Church, despite the significant cost to sponsor a child in the Guatemala program (due to Guatemalan government regulations), most, if not all, of the children in this program are sponsored.

The addition of the Guatemala program also taught us something else. God has demonstrated to us that He does not want us to go around shaking the trees trying to discover new opportunities for service. When I tried to stir up opportunities and contacts, not only did nothing come of it, I never even got a response from anyone. In contrast, when we sat back and waited for God to bring us an opportunity for service, everything fell into place perfectly when He put that opportunity directly on the path in front of us. With the exception of our Haiti program, each and every program we currently have has come to us in exactly the same way. Someone we already know and trust has come to us to tell us about a pastor or a Christian ministry in another country that can use the kind of help we can provide. This intermediary person already knows the ministry in need and can verify their legitimacy, so we can trust that these opportunities for service are ones we should pursue.

In fact, we have such confidence in God's direction in this manner that when a new opportunity for service is presented to us, rather than ask ourselves if there is a good reason to say yes to this opportunity, we ask ourselves if there is a good reason to say *no*. This is because we strongly believe if God is going to place an opportunity for service directly on the path in front of us, then He intends for us to be obedient and walk in it unless He reveals some compelling reason why we shouldn't.

Well-meaning people have often asked us why we would continue to accept new opportunities for service when we have many children (and adults) in our existing programs that are still waiting for a sponsor. The truth is, sponsorship is very fluid. On one day we may have every child in a particular program sponsored, while the next day something may happen in the life of a sponsor that causes them to have to discontinue their sponsorship. The idea that we would ever have every child (and adult) in every program sponsored is an ideal to strive for but not one which is attainable for any appreciable amount of time.

The real answer to this well-meaning question is simple. If God brings it to us, we believe He wants us to walk in it. He knows about the children and adults in the existing programs who are still waiting to be sponsored. For reasons we may never be able to explain, He has brought us new opportunities and has made it very clear that these are more of the good works He has prepared for us beforehand, and we need to walk in them.

Please don't misunderstand – I would not necessarily apply this guiding principle to any other ministry. I know there are many ministries that pursue opportunities to serve rather than wait for God to bring the opportunities to them. For them, it could be exactly the way God wants them to function. However, He has clearly shown us that He wants us to wait and trust Him to bring us the opportunities He wants us to pursue. Most often, He will put a particular country on the heart of someone on our board of directors first, such as when our board member Lorraine told us she knew God was going to bring us to Indonesia one day, and then out of the blue, through an intermediary person, He did. But that's another story.

*Guatemala coordinator, Wendy, on our first
trip to Guatemala*

7

OUR PARTNERSHIPS

How did we get connected to our partners in all the other countries? The list is long, but we feel each one is an illustration of how God has perfectly orchestrated all our partnerships. At the risk of perhaps putting some of you to sleep (I still remember the days when I skipped out on the missionaries' slide shows), here goes.

January 2003 – Haiti: Chapter One explained how we became connected to our partners in Haiti. The funding for this program helps to provide for the children's educational expenses. Lorna Faircloth is the Haiti program coordinator, and Karen Lamb is her assistant and e-mail coordinator for the program.

May 2007 – East Africa: Chapter Four explained how we became connected to our partners in East Africa. The funding for this program helps to provide for the children's educational expenses. At the time of this writing, I am the East Africa program coordinator.

December 2009 – Guatemala: Chapter Six explained how we became connected to our partner in Guatemala. The funding for this program helps to provide for the children's educational expenses. Wendy Marchand is the Guatemala program coordinator.

June 2010 – India, February 2011 - Philippines-Luzon: In June of 2010, we made our first trip to meet Pastor SJ Michael in India. In February of 2011, we made our first trip to meet with all our partners who are part of His Hands Christian Community Outreach Association on the island of Luzon in the Philippines. Both of these opportunities for service were brought to us by Nancy Millar. Nancy and I had met in online forums for people involved in sponsorship, and she had sponsored a child or two with our ministry. For many years, Nancy and her mother, Irene, put together hundreds of Christmas shoeboxes for Samaritan's Purse. Nancy enjoyed putting letters inside the shoeboxes she prepared and, as a result, established contact with several people overseas. She was trying to help these friends she had made, but, at the time, she was trying to do it on her own, and it was difficult. She asked us to consider taking on Pastor Michael and her friends in the Philippines (who later formed HHCCOA), and the rest is history. Pastor Michael has an after-school tutoring program for children in his area. HHCCOA helps the children in their ministries with school supplies and food distributions. Nancy later established her own ministry called United with Hope, which helps children in India and Malawi.[1] Rachael Santaniello is the program coordinator for the India program, and Clemma Nichols is the program coordinator for the Philippines-Luzon program. (Clemma is also an integral part of our finance team.)

Summer 2010 – Eswatini: His Hands for Eswatini (formerly Swaziland) was started in 2010 after being contacted by a friend from college, Barb Halvorson, asking if we could help a children's home there. The home had previously been receiving help from another organization but, due to a change in leadership within the other organization, their relationship had ended and they needed help. This is the only program we started without visiting the partner first, and it only happened because of our long-term and trusted relationship with Barb. In December of 2011, we finally made our first visit there to meet Thabsile Thwala and the children of The Fortress: a home for children who have been rescued from difficult domestic circumstances. Thabsile's ministry has also started helping children who attend feeding programs by providing the funds they need for their education. Jamie Dennett is the program coordinator for the Eswatini program.

July 2011 – Indonesia: Our partnership with Frankie and Marinka Portier and The Lion King orphanage in Bali, Indonesia, came about rather like our East Africa and Guatemala partnerships, only this time it was board member, Lorraine, who felt God would be leading us to Indonesia. Lorraine and I were in a van on our way home from the airport on a trip to Haiti when I received a call from my daughter, Kirstin. She asked me if we would be willing to help an orphanage on the island of Bali. A man from her church had been supporting them for years but was unable to continue and was looking for another organization to take over. I said we would look into it, not even realizing then that Bali was a part of Indonesia. Imagine Lorraine's surprise when I called her the next day, after looking up Bali online, and asked her to guess where Bali was! In July of 2011, we made our first visit there and established the sponsorship program, which helps provide funding for both the children's living expenses and their educational expenses. At the time of this writing, I am the Indonesia program coordinator.

November 2012 – Honduras: In August of 2012, we sent a team (including myself) to visit our partners in Guatemala. On our final flight into the airport in Guatemala City, our flight experienced *two* failed landing attempts. It was a stormy night with lightning flashing all around the aircraft, and the airport is surrounded by mountains, making the landing challenging. The first time, when the jet was just about to touch down, the pilot had to pull up suddenly, causing the aircraft to shake terribly. As he circled the airport to try again, he told us he would make another attempt, and if it wasn't successful, we would have to divert to another airport. As the jet descended a second time, the landing gear actually touched down, but the aircraft bounced back up, and the pilot quickly pulled up again. The jet was considerably unhappier with that move than it had been the first time, and there was silence on board as everyone prayed it would hold together. We survived, and the passengers erupted in shouts of enthusiasm when the pilot announced we would have to divert to Cancun. It was a Saturday night, and some of the passengers had visions of partying the night away in that hot spot.

After some time had passed, the pilot's voice came over the intercom again, and he announced they "couldn't get anyone on the phone in Cancun," so we would have to divert to San Pedro Sula instead. I noticed many of the passengers, including myself, reaching for the airline magazine in the seat pocket to look at the map and figure out where in the world San Pedro Sula was! We discovered it was in Honduras – a country I had never been to before but had dreamed about for years.

We refueled in San Pedro Sula and then headed back to Guatemala City, where we finally landed safely. As we exited the plane, the pilot stood beside the exit door, a little pale, apologizing to each of us as we got off. After we returned to the U.S. from that trip, I found an email waiting for me in my inbox. It was from a sweet woman named Lori Hughes. She had gotten my name from a long-time ministry volunteer and dear friend, Karen Lamb, who went to the same church as Lori in San Diego, California. Lori had been helping pastors in Honduras and wanted our help to begin a sponsorship program to help those pastors care for the children in their churches. Here's the God-ordained point of this long-winded story. Those pastors are located in the area around San Pedro Sula in Honduras. I just smiled when I read that in her email. In November of 2012, we sent a team to Honduras, and His Hands for Honduras was formed. Lori Hughes is the coordinator of the Honduras program, and the funding provides for the children's school expenses and food for a feeding program for them. It also provides funding for monthly food distributions for the elderly.

June 2013 – His Hands for the Dominican Republic: In June of 2013, His Hands for the Dominican Republic was formed after we received a request for help for two churches in the Dominican Republic. That request came from Empowering Action[2] – a ministry founded by Kent Husted. At that time, Kent attended the same church as our daughter, Kirstin. Kent knew of His Hands for some time before an actual partnership could be formed with us, so we were all thrilled when God finally made it happen. A year or two after the program was initially set up with those two original churches, a third ministry – Colegio Moriah – was added to the program as well. All three ministries provide for the children's educational costs. Sheila Johnson is the Dominican program coordinator.

November 2014 – His Hands for Mexico: Fayette Baptist Church in Fayette, Maine, has been one of our supporting churches for years. They had an existing relationship with Franco and Barby Mendez, Mexican missionaries who are working in the mountain community of Cuautotola, Mexico. Associate Pastor at Fayette Baptist, Henry Cooper, who oversees Missions at Fayette Baptist and later became the vice president of our board of directors, asked us to partner with Franco and Barby to help them with the support they needed for their children's program, including providing funding for children to attend school. In November of 2014, we sent a team to visit with Franco and Barby on the coldest mission trip I've ever been on, and His Hands for Mexico was formed. Jenna Blakey is the Mexico program coordinator.

June 2017 – His Hands for Myanmar: In the summer of 2016, Pastor Steve Gammon, brother of board member and long-time volunteer Marilee Colpitts, met Pastor Go[3] at a denominational conference in Orlando, Florida. He learned about Pastor Go's efforts to minister to children and his children's home and felt convicted to do something to help him. Eventually he talked with his sister, Marilee, and asked if His Hands would be willing to take on the support of Pastor Go. In June of 2017, Steve, along with a small team from His Hands, went to visit Pastor Go in Myanmar, and His Hands for Myanmar was created. The funds from this program help provide for both the living expenses and the educational expenses of the children in the children's home run by Pastor Go. Rachael Santaniello is the Myanmar program coordinator.

January 2018 – His Hands for Nicaragua:

Back in July of 2013, Mike Bell was sent to Central America by the first international organization he worked with to investigate several opportunities for service. (This is how his present organization became involved with our partners in Honduras, where both our ministries are serving in cooperation with one another.) In the course of that trip, he visited a pastor in the mountains of Nicaragua, Pastor Carlos Baez, and was impressed with the work he was doing there with special needs children. However, the organization Mike was working with decided not to pursue a partnership with Pastor Carlos. Fast forward to 2017, during the time period when Mike was working on the formation of Healing Nations, and we had a phone conversation in which he mentioned he planned to return to Nicaragua and pursue a partnership with Pastor Carlos. He asked us if we would be interested in partnering with Pastor Carlos as well. In January of 2018, we sent a team to Nicaragua to meet with Pastor Carlos, and His Hands for Nicaragua was formed. The funding for this program helps provide monthly food bags for the families of special needs children. Jessi Culyer is the Nicaragua program coordinator.

January 2018 – His Hands for the Philippines-Cebu: At about the same time I was having discussions with Mike Bell about Nicaragua, I received a phone call from another sweet lady from California named Laurie Hughes. She is not the same person who asked us about helping the pastors in Honduras (Lori Hughes), but they do share a similar name. This is because they are sisters-in-law! Laurie's church, Liberty Church in Fairfield, California, had an existing relationship with The CURE Foundation on the island of Cebu in the Philippines. The CURE Foundation has a home for young girls who have been rescued out of child sex trafficking, and she asked me if His Hands would consider partnering with them to try to bring in some much-needed support. In January of 2018, His Hands for the Philippines-Cebu was formed when Laurie visited The CURE Foundation with a team from her church and gathered the information we needed on the girls. The funding for this program helps to provide for both the girls' living expenses as well as their education and counseling. Laurie Hughes is the Philippines-Cebu program coordinator.

April 2018 – His Hands for Brazil: Going back to sunny San Diego, California, and our sweet program coordinator, Lori Hughes, who in early 2018 contacted me and said she had a friend in her church who came from the country of Brazil. He had approached her and asked if it would be possible to set up a program to help the pastor of his church back in Brazil, Pastor Roberto Naves Amorim, who has a children's ministry in a slum area outside his city. In April of 2018, we sent a team to Brazil, and His Hands for Brazil was started. The funding for this program helps to provide educational materials and food for the children's ministry meetings and also provides for some of their school supplies. Ray Hutchinson is the Brazil program coordinator.

June 2018 – His Hands for Kenya: In 2018, Mike Bell talked to us about a pastor he had met in Kenya while working with his previous organization. The name of this pastor is Bishop Richard Ogol, and he has a ministry providing help to widows in his area. Mike asked us if we would be willing to join up with Bishop Ogol to help bring some relief to these widows. In June of 2018, we sent a team to Kenya to gather information on the widows, and children who needed assistance to go to school, and His Hands for Kenya was established. The funding for this program helps to provide food assistance and other material needs for the widows as well as funds for the children's educational expenses. Shelly Zoebisch is the Kenya program coordinator.

July 2018 – His Hands for Cuba: In another one of my phone conversations with Mike Bell, the subject of Cuba came up. Mike mentioned that he had a friend and ministry partner, Leticia Acosta Aguiar, who has a ministry called Arms of Love Ministry,[4] which serves as a support & resource hub for serving God in Cuba. Before too long, Mike was calling me again to tell me Leticia had contact with a pastor in Cuba who was running a nursing home and could use our help. In April of 2018, Philip and I joined a team going to Cuba with Leticia that included Mike Bell and his family. That trip laid the groundwork for a follow-up trip Philip and I made to Cuba in July of 2018 when we gathered the necessary information on the elderly people in the nursing home of Pastor Vidal Felipe Hernandez Villas and His Hands for Cuba was started. The funding for this program helps provide for the physical needs of the elderly people in the nursing home. Cherry Martin is the Cuba program coordinator.

August 2018 – His Hands for South Africa: In May of 2018, we had a team of four in East Africa: our friend Pam Brochu and her husband, Luke, along with my husband, Philip, and me. We were in Rwanda spending time with our partner there, Pastor Jean Rudasumbwa, who is a co-worker of Pastor Bamo. Normally we would stay at a particular mission compound in Kigali, but when Pastor Jean tried to make a reservation for us to stay there he discovered it was fully booked. He had to book us into a different mission compound where we had never stayed.

There weren't many other people staying there at the time, so the facility was pretty empty.

They had a large, common dining hall where meals were served, and we found ourselves sitting there all by ourselves. Then another small group of men came in to have dinner. They sat at a table very close to ours and soon we were chatting with each other. We joined our tables together and began to share about how God was using all of us there in Rwanda. Our conversations were a wonderful demonstration of how the body of Christ is one body, no matter where God had us living and serving. We marveled at how God had orchestrated our meeting since we normally wouldn't be staying at that compound. In their group was Pastor Theo Burakeye, from South Africa, and his friend and co-laborer in the ministry, David Cheeks, from Kentucky in the U.S. We spent several meals talking with each other and enjoying sweet fellowship. Then, one evening, Pastor Theo asked us why we had never visited South Africa. I told him it was because no one had ever asked us to come. His response was simple – "Is that all it takes?" Then David asked us if we would come to South Africa to see Pastor Theo's children's ministry for the children of families living in a squatters' camp and consider partnering with him to help bring in support. In August of 2018, we sent a team to South Africa, and His Hands for South Africa was formed. The funding for this program helps to provide for the educational costs and food for the children in their daycare and preschool program. At the time of this writing, Kristine Chamberlain is the South Africa program coordinator.

August 2018 – His Hands for Liberia: At our annual coordinators' retreat in the fall of 2017, long-time ministry volunteer and program coordinator, Wendy

Marchand, approached me about the possibility of exploring an opportunity for service in the country of Liberia. At that time, she had a relative who was stationed at the U.S. Embassy in Monrovia. Through the ambassador, he learned of a children's home outside of Monrovia. He and some of the marines at the embassy began to visit there. They brought them help in the form of tangible items like toys, school supplies, clothing, etc. He knew his time at the embassy was limited, so he had asked Wendy if His Hands would consider partnering with the children's home. In August of 2018, we sent a team to Liberia to meet with Pastor Sam Kargbo, and His Hands for Liberia began. The funding for this program helps to provide for both the children's living expenses and their educational expenses. Nichole Appleby is the Liberia program coordinator.

January 2019 – His Hands for Tanzania: Board member and volunteer, Marilee Colpitts, has a sister, Cheryl Tyler, who frequently spends several months a year in Israel. In 2018 she was in Israel and met a woman whose daughter and son-in-law were living in Tanzania running a children's home they had started. The daughter was very sick with cancer and passed away in October of 2018, leaving her husband, Jerry Backus, to run the home of 80+ children on his own as well as raising the four Tanzanian children they had adopted. He definitely needed help. Cheryl asked Marilee if His Hands would consider partnering with Jerry Backus and Falco's Children's Home, and we sent a team there in January of 2019 to establish His Hands for Tanzania. The funding for this program helps to provide for both the children's living expenses and their educational expenses. Bonnie Bennett is the Tanzania program coordinator.

There you have it. If you have made it this far, I

congratulate you for your patience and curiosity. Each partnership is precious to us because it represents another piece of the body of Christ coming together to work in unity to the praise and glory of our Lord and Savior. Thank you for taking the time to go through all this!

Mike and Joani Bell (right) visiting with one of the elderly ladies in the Cuba program

II

———————

HIS STORIES

8

WHAT WE REALLY DO

"It must be so exciting traveling around the world getting to see all kinds of new things"!

"There are plenty of people right here in the U.S. who need help. Why aren't you helping any of them?"

"It must make you feel so good to do the things you're doing!"

These and other questions or comments about our work come up frequently. While we understand most people ask these questions from a place of curiosity, they reflect an inaccurate view of exactly what it is God has us doing. These questions do have answers, but they might not be the answers you would expect. I am going to start with the first one.

Yes, it can be exciting traveling to new and exotic places. However, most of the places God sends us are places most people wouldn't want to go. I'm not sure I've ever heard someone say they'd love to go on vacation in the Democratic Republic of the Congo or Liberia. And the reason we're going to these places is not to experience something new and exotic. We're going to visit our partners and the people involved in their ministries. For us, it's about strengthening our existing relationships and starting new ones. It's about investing our lives into theirs and trying to understand the differences and similarities in our cultures so we can do the things God has for us to do in a way that works in their culture. It's wonderful when we receive messages from our partners like the one I received while I was writing this; "Dear God, Thank you very much for the good friends You have given for us in the other side of the earth."

It's also about checking up on the people who are benefitting from our sponsorship programs to make sure they are still involved, and they are receiving what they're supposed to receive. Yes, occasionally, we are treated to fun or exciting experiences, but that's not why we do what we do, and it can never be a motivating factor for us if we're going to do things in a way that's pleasing to God. Also, to be frank, when you have to make several trips like this in a year, it becomes exhausting, not exciting.

Yes, we acknowledge and agree there are plenty of people in need right here in the U.S. If someone is asking us that question, it would make sense to assume they are aware of the needs in the U.S. too. So our response to this question is this: "Yes, there are people here in the U.S. who need help. So what are you doing to help them?" This may seem like a snide response, but hear me out. Speaking personally, when I have been asked this question, it has been very clear that the one doing the asking isn't really concerned with the needs of people in the U.S. on a personal level. They are more interested in pointing out an assumed flaw in the way we operate since it appears we are more concerned about people in other countries than we are about people living right here in our cities, our towns, and our neighborhoods.

Nothing could be further from the truth. We care about people in need no matter where they live. We are concerned about children who lack what they need to be able to attend school. We are concerned about elderly people who are lonely and hungry. Most importantly, we are even more concerned when any of these people don't know or understand that God loves them more than any of us ever could.

You may be asking, "So if this is true, why don't you have a program to address the needs of people here in the U.S.?" The answer to that is simple. God has not brought us an opportunity to serve a partner here in the U.S. If the day comes when He puts an opportunity in front of us to help a partner ministry in the United States, we will handle it the same way we handle those opportunities for service which come from outside the U.S. We will ask the right questions; do the necessary investigative work to see if our model will fit their need, and if God keeps that path of service wide open to us, we'll walk in it.

Yes, there are times when we do feel good about what we do. But there are also many times when we don't. As Philip has often said, "We don't do good to feel good about doing good. Because sometimes it doesn't feel good." If our feelings were the motivation behind what we do, we would have quit a long time ago. It doesn't feel good when we see a baby who has been badly burned in a fire, watching them suffer and breathe their last breath because we are helpless to do anything to prevent that outcome. It doesn't feel good when we learn that a young girl in the program has been sold for sex by a parent, and the parent won't let her attend school anymore.[1] It doesn't feel good when our partners have been successfully helping a child, bringing her to the point of thriving, only to have her disappear when her neglectful and abusive parent takes her out of town, and they can't be traced. It doesn't feel good when we have to contact a sponsor to tell them the child they sponsor has died. It doesn't feel good when our partners go through wars, natural disasters, face health crises, or even die, and we are powerless to help.

It didn't feel good when we met identical twin boys in the Philippines who were both disabled, seeing them struggle while watching their mother, and then their aunt, try to care for them without knowing what might be wrong with them. It didn't feel good going to the hospital with one of the boys and his aunt, listening to the doctor confirm their suspicions saying the boy had muscular dystrophy and nothing could be done to prevent his decline. It didn't feel good realizing that, since the boys were identical twins and muscular dystrophy is a genetic disorder, then his brother was obviously dealing with the same thing and would face the same outcome. It didn't feel good when we heard about the death of one of the boys just a few short years later. And it felt devastating seeing the remaining boy one last time, seeing how much his condition had declined, and realizing this would be the last time I would see him on this side of Glory. It felt incredibly tragic kissing his cheek one last time and telling his aunt she had done an incredible job caring for him and his brother, knowing no amount of excellent care would save the remaining boy from dying just a few weeks after I said my last good-bye to him.

None of that feels good, but it's part of the deal. Building relationships opens us up to all kinds of hurt. We wouldn't have it any other way.

Here's the real truth. The overwhelming majority of what we do is done sitting in front of a computer in our own homes. Traveling is a very small piece of the assignment

God has given us. The coordinators might only travel once a year or once every eighteen months, depending on which program God has given them. Then they spend the rest of the year doing the mundane, repetitive tasks of keeping lists, typing up information, editing photos, keeping the website current, answering emails, facilitating communication, promoting and doing presentations, and on and on and on.

Our treasurer, Wanda Meisner, and the other finance department volunteers, work tirelessly processing the funds we receive. They are making lists and sending funds to our partners regularly, answering questions from sponsors and other donors, and keeping our accounts current. None of that is glamourous or exciting, but it's the vital work that keeps the ministry going. Most of what gets done isn't noticed unless it's done wrong. There's no one standing behind us praising or encouraging us when we type that information sheet or update that information on the website or record that donation coming in. However, we do hear about it when mistakes are made. We don't always get to see a positive outcome from our efforts. It's not always exciting, and it doesn't usually make us feel good, but that's okay with us because it's the assignment we've been given, and we do it all for His glory.

> "And whatever you do, do it heartily, as to the Lord and not to men, knowing that from the Lord you will receive the reward of the inheritance; for you serve the Lord Christ." (Colossians 3:23-24 NKJV)

Some of our program coordinators working together during one of our annual coordinators' retreats (left to right – Wanda, Lori, Sheila, Jenna, Lorna, and Sherlyn)

9

THE LORD'S PLAN

"Do you always take on every opportunity for service that's presented to you? Do they all work out?"

The short answer to that is no. The longer answer is a bit more involved, as you will soon read.

The first opportunity presented to us that didn't work out was in Indonesia. We had been asked to investigate opportunities to help two different children's homes on the island of Bali. The first one was on the south side of the island, near the airport, so on our initial trip we went to that children's home first. We visited there and got the basic details about the home, met the director, met the children, and talked about how the sponsorship program would work. The director said he wanted some time to think about it, and we agreed. We still had to go visit The Lion King on the north side of Bali and would be coming back to the south side before we had to leave. We arranged to come back and check-in with the director before we left and would get his final answer at that time.

When we returned, fully expecting to start gathering the necessary information on the children, we were surprised to hear the director say he had decided he did not want to participate. He had concerns the children might lose respect for him as their father-figure if he had to ask other people for help to support them. We respected his decision and thanked him for allowing us to visit and returned to the U.S. a bit confused about why God would send us there only to have him say no. However, a few years later, we learned that he had been asked to leave the children's home, and the implications were very negative. We never heard any of the specifics, but we were very thankful God had not allowed us to get involved there.

Another time we were asked to help a children's ministry in Mexico. We had friends who were going to visit the ministry, so we agreed to go along and see about starting a partnership with the director. We made the trip, and everything looked good, so we gathered the necessary information on the children involved in that ministry. We also spent quite some time talking to the director explaining how everything would work concerning the sponsorships, including the fact that information would be put on our website. We are very sensitive to the issues our partners face, so we always discuss the website with them to determine what info is safe to share and what info is not safe. When we left there, we felt as though we had worked through all those details to everyone's satisfaction. We went back to the U.S. and got busy. We got the website set up, added all the children's information, and got everything ready to launch. Once everything was done, we contacted the director to let him know we were ready to launch the site, and he asked us to wait.

After a short waiting period, he got back to us and said he had changed his mind and didn't want to participate. He had concerns about their security with information being posted online. We told him we understood and gave up on that specific program. Just a few short years later, we learned the director had passed away and there were some negative implications being discussed. Again, we have no idea what those negative things might have been, or if they were true, but we were still very thankful God had stopped our involvement there. Not long after, God brought us another opportunity in a different part of Mexico where we did establish a program with an amazing partner, and it's still flourishing today.

Another organization actually started the first program we had in Kenya. The administration of that particular program then passed through more than one other organization over the years. We were asked to take over when the current leadership needed to retire. It was a program I had known about for years and had even sponsored a child for a while, so it seemed like a reasonable request. After discussing it with our board and with some other key people we wanted to have involved, we decided to take it on. It was difficult to do because some of the existing sponsors were not happy having another organization take over the administration, especially an organization that was clearly a Christian one. Things were a bit rough, but we were willing to continue because we knew the children needed help.

After a year or two, we were approached by another organization that had ties to the school receiving the aid, and those ties pre-dated our involvement. They asked us if we would mind if they enrolled some of the children in their program too. We would work together transparently, so children were not duplicated in both sponsorship programs, which sounded very reasonable. After some time to consider and pray, we realized it would make much more sense to simply turn it all over to this other organization. They were more than happy to take on the whole thing, and the existing sponsors were happier to have a different organization responsible for it. We transferred it all over to this new organization, and everyone was happy. Before too long, God brought us a different opportunity to serve in Kenya with another amazing partner. We were happy to establish a new Kenya program with him and his ministry.

There have been times when we have added new programs and it has taken a very long time for the children (or adults) to begin being sponsored. To be honest, we can start to have doubts when this happens because we can't always understand why one program takes off quickly while another one can languish – sometimes for years. We have to remind ourselves that the outcome is not up to us. God only asks us to be obedient and walk in the good works He's put in front of us and then simply trust Him for the outcome. It is difficult, though - especially when the children or our partners are struggling with the outcome even more than we are.

We frequently receive requests for help from people we don't know in places where we have no reliable contacts, and they're asking for help for their own ministry or organization. As difficult as it is for us to ignore these requests, we have no other option. We have no way of knowing if the ministries in question are legitimate, and we do not have the time or the financial resources to investigate them to find out. Beyond that, God has already shown us the pattern He has established for us. All the opportunities He's brought to fruition for our ministry have come from someone we already know and trust who is asking us to help someone else, not themselves. It's only those opportunities that we'll even take the time to investigate.

We have had many opportunities come to us the right way that have never panned out. In some cases, we have not been able to work out the details in a way that would fit our model. In other cases, we have never been able to visit to see things for ourselves and see if our model will work. Some of these opportunities involved ministries in closed countries where our potential partners have felt it would not be safe – either for them or for us – to make a visit. Some opportunities have come to us, and we've discussed them, coming to the conclusion that our model will work for them. Then we have to wait until we can make the arrangements for a visit. At the time of this writing, we have one potential new partner who is still waiting for us to come, but we can't make a visit for the foreseeable future due to the Covid-19 pandemic.

There are often specific countries on the heart of someone in our leadership, but without any concrete opportunity to serve, as I have already discussed. This can be the hardest time of all to wait: when one of us has an overwhelming desire to help children (or adults) in a specific country, but God has not yet brought us an opportunity to serve in that country. We know God's plan is for us to simply wait, and pray, for Him to bring that desire to fruition. That can be a lot easier said than done.

"Many are the plans in a person's heart, but it is the Lord's purpose that prevails." (Proverbs 19:21 NIV)

Jamie Dennett with some children in Kampala, Uganda

10

HOW TO DO WHAT WE DO

"It must be so hard to go to these poor countries and see so much need. How can you do that and not want to bring them all the things they need or bring them home with you?"

A typhoon stranded a monkey on an island. In a protected place on the shore, while waiting for the raging waters to recede, he spotted a fish swimming against the current. It seemed to the monkey that the fish was struggling and needed assistance. Being of kind heart, the monkey resolved to help the fish. A tree leaned precariously over the spot where the fish seemed to be struggling. At considerable risk to himself, the monkey moved far out on a limb, reached down, and snatched the fish from the waters. Scurrying back to the safety of his shelter, he carefully laid the fish on dry ground. For a few moments, the fish showed excitement but soon settled into a peaceful rest. Joy and satisfaction

swelled inside the monkey. He had successfully
helped another creature. — An Old Eastern Parable

Over the years, we have learned many things the hard
way. As a result of learning those lessons, we now instruct
all our teams, especially those "newbies" on each team,
telling them to be "quick to listen, slow to speak, and slow to
act." In scripture, in the book of James, we're given a similar
instruction, but it ends with "slow to *anger*." We've taken a
little liberty with that instruction by changing it up a bit,
but we still think it's a valuable piece of instruction for those
filled with zeal but not much experience. Sadly, in our zeal
to help, we can often cause more harm than good or end up
not doing any good at all. We refer to that as "being a
monkey."

One of our first examples of misplaced zeal happened
on our second trip to Haiti. On our first trip, Philip and
Davin had spent quite a bit of time playing soccer with
young boys in the street. In the area where they played, the
street was cobblestone with lots of trash, small rocks, broken
glass, bits of metal and concrete debris, etc. The Haitian
boys played with bare feet, causing us much concern for the
welfare of their feet.

In the time that passed between our first visit to Haiti
and our second, we came up with what we thought was a
great idea. We asked our church and other friends to donate
gently used sneakers we could take to Haiti to give to
children who needed them. We even took it a step further
and asked for socks since we figured the kids couldn't
possibly wear the sneakers without socks, right? By the time
we left for Haiti a year later, we had quite a large assortment
of both sneakers and socks for children in Terrier Rouge.

We had learned just enough on our first trip to be dangerous, but we at least knew we couldn't go out in the street and start handing out sneakers and socks, or we would most likely cause a riot. We carefully selected children we knew and would cautiously sneak them into the house, away from prying eyes, and find them a pair of sneakers and socks that would fit. Once we had them on their feet, we would send them back out with their new-to-them footwear on, figuring none of the other kids would even notice. It seemed to go well. There were no uprisings of children rushing the house demanding sneakers for themselves and their siblings. We were feeling pretty good about our plan and how smart we were.

Before the time came to play soccer, Philip and our son Jake (who had joined us on this trip) had found several of the boys who played the previous year and had managed to give them sneakers and socks without being discovered. However, when they all gathered to play, none of the boys were wearing their new footwear. They were all playing barefoot. Philip asked them where their sneakers were and why they weren't wearing them. "Oh... we left them at home. We don't want to ruin them by playing soccer with them on." It seems we weren't so smart after all. We had observed the boys playing soccer and had come to our own American conclusion about what they needed rather than simply being quick to listen, slow to speak, and slow to act. Yes, it was helpful for them to have a new pair of shoes, but our intentions had been to provide something for them to wear while playing soccer, a need that, for them, didn't exist.

On this same trip, my friend Pam was a team leader again. A group of us had walked with her to the outskirts of town to see a man who made child-sized wooden chairs. We were interested in purchasing some from him and went to talk to him. The legs and the rungs of the chairs were whittled by hand at the joints, so there were quite a lot of wood shavings on the ground around his home.

While we were standing there talking with him, a very old woman came by and was picking up handfuls of those wood shavings. The man who made the chairs told us she came by a lot and picked up as many wood shavings as she could so she could use them for a cooking fire. Pam's heart went out to this incredibly skinny, ancient old woman, but she knew she couldn't simply walk over to her and give her money. There were people around who would see what she was doing, and this could cause a lot of trouble for everyone. Pam waited until no one was paying attention and cautiously snuck over to the old woman and discreetly slipped a dollar into her hand. She tried to be inconspicuous, but it's almost impossible to accomplish that in Haiti, and some young boys saw what happened. They didn't see the money, but they figured out what had taken place, and they started to go after this ancient woman, trying to get the money from her. We were all horrified, but the chair maker intervened and managed to get the boys to go away so the woman could get home safely. We went back to the mission house feeling terrible about the whole situation but didn't see how we could do anything more to help her.

After we went back to the U.S., Pam couldn't get this sweet old woman out of her mind. When we put together our own team and returned to Haiti six months later, Pam gave us some money and asked us to find a way to use it to help the woman. Once back in Haiti, we knew we couldn't just go find her and give it to her, but we wanted to at least find out if she was still alive. She was the skinniest human being we had ever seen. She appeared to be as old as Methuselah, so we knew we shouldn't assume she was still living.

We had someone take us to that same area of the village, and we managed to find her house. Sure enough, she was still alive. But there was absolutely no way we could give her any money with so many people around trying to figure out why the "blancs"[1] had come to see her. We left and started to walk back to the mission house, brainstorming while we walked. We thought about simply going to the market and using the money Pam gave us to buy food and bring it to the old woman. We soon realized that wouldn't work either. There was no way we could go to the market, buy her some food, and then walk over to her house with sacks of beans and rice without people noticing and following us.

We ended up back at the mission house feeling frustrated and defeated. Then we finally got smart. We asked our Haitian hostess, Marie, what we should do. "If you trust me to take care of the money, I will take it and change it into Haitian currency. Then I will have her come to my house, and I'll give her a small amount every week until it's gone. I will only give her coins and not paper money because she probably wouldn't know how much the paper money was worth, and I'll only give her enough to buy just enough food for each week until the money is gone." *Bingo!* The perfect answer to our dilemma! Then we noticed Marie had tears gathering in her eyes, so we asked her what was wrong. She said, "It is such a blessing for me when I can help my own people. I don't often have the possibility to do that, so I am very thankful you will trust me with this money and give me the possibility to help her."

There it is: the perfect solution. Not only does it

address our desire, and Pam's desire, to help someone who desperately needs help, but it provides the help in a way that will actually be helpful and not cause more harm than good. Plus, the icing on the cake is that it's a blessing for Marie to play a role in blessing the woman, whose name, we learned, was Zouzoune.

Marie had Zouzoune come to the house so she could tell her about our plan. Zouzoune lifted up her dress to show us her sunken belly, and we couldn't help but notice she didn't even have underwear. She had to wrap rags around herself to cover that part of her body. She told us she was one hundred and three years old, was born in the Dominican Republic, and came to Haiti with her parents when she was a young girl to escape the persecution of Haitians taking place at that time in the D.R. She was so happy, vivacious, and full of life! It was a blessing to get to know her and become a part of her life until she died several years later. Between all of us who had met her and came to love her, we managed to keep giving Marie money for Zouzoune until she passed. Such a joy it was to hear her exclaim, "Ai Yi Yi!!" whenever she was overcome with emotion, revealing her Dominican roots. What an amazing woman leading an amazing, but difficult, life and I look forward to meeting up with her again at His throne.

Learning this lesson and other similar lessons has caused us to adopt a somewhat-controversial policy concerning bringing material goods with us on our trips. If someone offers us a donation of clothing or shoes or some other items, in most cases, we will graciously refuse the offer. We realize people have good intentions and simply want to help, but bringing things to give out often causes more harm than good. The example I like to use is this: let's say a sponsor wanted to give several crates of pencils to the school their sponsored child attends. It seems like a gracious offer because they're offering pencils to every child in the school, not just the child they personally sponsor. But what if the parents of their sponsored child have a stall in the market where they sell pencils? By giving every child in the school a pencil or two, has the sponsor really helped their sponsored child and their family, or have they caused them harm by taking away the need for the product they sell?

Other than in times of crisis when material goods might be in short supply, the places we visit have clothing, shoes, school supplies, food, etc., available in their markets. What the people lack is the money to purchase those items. When someone says they want to donate to help meet needs, our number one suggestion of something to donate is money. The money can be used to purchase the needed items in-country, which not only helps the recipients of the items that are purchased, but also helps the vendors who sell those items. In this way, everybody wins.

Going back to how we started this chapter, if the monkey really wants to help the fish, the best thing for him to do is to dive into the water and swim with the fish for a while. He needs to experience, as much as possible, what the fish's life is like. He needs to learn about fish culture. He may even discover that what he perceived as a need isn't really a need the fish has: like when we assumed the boys needed sneakers for playing soccer. The monkey needs to ask the fish if he really has a need and, if so, how he can truly help him. He needs to be quick to listen to the response of the fish but be slow to speak by not immediately promising to do everything the fish has asked. He needs to be slow to act on what the fish has said, taking time to pray and ask God to show him what he should do and the best way to go about doing it. All of this is done best in the context of relationship.

"Desire without knowledge is not good—how much more will hasty feet miss the way!...Listen to advice and accept discipline, and at the end you will be counted among the wise." (Proverbs 19:2, 20 NIV)

Zouzoune

11

IT MUST BE SO HARD

"Isn't it hard to listen to the children's stories? It must be so sad!"

Yes, it is. Sometimes it's encouraging, and sometimes it's downright funny. The only way we can handle it is to entrust them all to their heavenly Father, who cares for them and loves them more than we ever could. Here are just a few examples.

In most of the places we visit, the children will gather at a centralized location (or we will go to their school) where we will document their information. On one of our trips to the Philippines, instead of interviewing the children, I was tasked with photographing them. I truly enjoy that job because it can be a lot of fun interacting with the children trying to get a good smile out of them. That particular year, a little boy named Micah was sitting next to me, watching the whole process. He was about four years old and had recently come to live with his new family, Pastor Chris and his family, after losing his biological family in a typhoon in the southern Philippines. Pastor Chris had gone there to help after the typhoon, had met Micah, and decided to add

Micah to their family. As one of the other pastors described him, Micah was a lively boy. This is very apt description for him because even with the terrible loss he had gone through; his cheerful, energetic spirit remained. He was a lot of fun. Watching me photograph the children, Micah soon observed that I gave a small lollipop to each child after they were finished having their photo taken. I could just see the thoughts running through his mind about how much he was going to enjoy his lollipop when it was finally his turn.

The wait was proving difficult, and he began to get more and more fidgety. Finally, he leaned over towards me, cupped his hands around his mouth, and whispered, "I want to tell you something." So I leaned over, curious to hear what he had to say to me. "You are *so* beautiful!" I laughed out loud, hearing those sweet words out of a little four-year-old boy. He had obviously figured out the best way to get a lollipop from a lady was to compliment her. But I didn't give in. I just thanked him and kept right on working, photographing the other children. Finally, Micah's turn came, and he sat down in the photo chair with the biggest grin on his face. I didn't even have to try to get a smile out of him. He couldn't have smiled any bigger if he had tried. I snapped his photo, told him he was done and handed him his long-awaited lollipop. He somehow managed to grin even more, jumped down from the platform, and started to skip away. Then, suddenly he stopped, hurried back over to where I was sitting, and planted a kiss on my cheek before running away again. What a charmer!

In Haiti, the little ones are petrified of our light-colored skin. They scream and run away when they see us walking down the street. You can imagine some of the difficult situations we find ourselves in when we try to document them for the sponsorship program. There was one little boy whose reaction was pretty amusing. He was in the three-year-old class in the preschool when the director brought him to me to be interviewed. The little ones are too little to answer the questions, so a teacher, or the director, will stay with them and give us the answers. I was asking the questions, and the director was answering while the little guy just stood there beside the table, not paying attention to anything that was happening. He was perfectly content until he glanced up and saw me sitting right next to him. Instead of screaming as most kids do, he was perfectly silent, but his little legs apparently turned to jelly. He flopped down on the floor and just laid there. He hadn't fainted; he was just so petrified at the thought of standing next to a light-skinned person that his legs gave out. The director bent over and helped him back up, and he stood there, just fine until he looked up at me again. *Flop!* Those legs turned to jelly again, and down he went. We finished the interview, and the director helped him up and walked him over to Jess, who would take him to be measured. The little boy was fine until he looked up to see who was taking him. *Flop!*

During the interviews we hear some amusing answers: like the child who attends the Baptist church but says they want to be a priest or a nun when they grow up, or attends the Catholic church but says they want to be a pastor when they grow up. Some children say they don't like science, but want to be doctors, and some children don't like math, but want to be accountants. There was one little girl in Haiti who, surprisingly, wasn't afraid of our light-colored skin even though she was still quite young. As I interviewed her, she didn't speak but would shake her head "yes" or "no" or hold up the appropriate number of fingers in response to my questions. I asked her if she had brothers and sisters, and she nodded her little head, "yes." I then asked her how many brothers, then how many sisters, and she held up three fingers each time. I noticed the teachers were sitting in the back of the room laughing. I asked them to confirm the numbers, and they roared with laughter, saying, "She doesn't have any siblings at all!"

Probably the funniest interview I've ever participated in was during one of our Haiti trips. Long-time volunteer and board member Matt and I were both doing interviews at the same time while sitting at opposite ends of the same table. Things were going fine until I became aware of some difficulty Matt was having with his interview. He was interviewing a little girl, about seven years old, and was having trouble with her response to one of the questions. We were both interviewing in Creole, and even though Matt spoke Creole very well, he leaned over to me and asked me if I could stop for a minute and listen to what she was saying. He thought he knew what she had said, but he wanted to be sure and asked me to confirm it.

He asked her what her father did for work. As she answered his question, her voice had a little sing-song lilt to it. She bobbed her head from side to side and did a little swoop of her hand as she counted on her fingers three different things: (swoop up with one finger) "He plants a garden" (swoop up with two fingers) "He pushes a wheelbarrow" (swoop up with three fingers) "And he's a *thief*!" She was very pleased with herself and with her answer, then skipped over to the measuring station when she was done. We continued interviewing the next children in line, but we did see her again as she started to walk out of the building after having her photo done. Before she reached the door, she stopped, ran back to me, and in a very excited voice, she said, "I'm done! Bye, teacher!" What a hoot!

Before I give you the wrong impression and lead you to believe it's all sunshine and roses, there are far more heartbreaking moments. For example, measuring a child's feet only to discover their socks are several sizes too big and stiff from being worn repeatedly without washing them. Then, noticing their shoes are two sizes too small as we try to force them back on with all that extra sock material wadded up inside. Another example is weighing a child and discovering they are severely underweight for their age. Also, having a secondary student, who's been watching Philip measure kids for most of the day, lean over and ask him how long he had to go to school to learn how to do that. Another one is trying to make a child presentable before taking their photo. This means you have to wipe their face and try to tuck in their clothing when it's missing buttons and vital zippers or is torn, dirty, and tattered. Having an older boy step on the scale after taking off his shoes - the ones he was wearing without socks – and leaving a black footprint on the scale. We had to scrub it to get it clean again. It breaks our hearts seeing the children in the Congo with open sores all over their legs and feet with flies swarming around them. It is so hard to see the condition of some of these children.

As hard as it is to see the condition of their little bodies, hearing some of the situations in which they're living, or from which they have been removed, will rip your heart out. Like the little girl in Haiti who very matter-of-factly told us about the situation in her home. She was living with her mother and her grandmother and many, many other children who were half-siblings of hers. They were not children of her mother. They were children of her father, who had many other women around town with whom he had produced children. When one of these ladies would give birth, he would take the baby and bring it to his wife – the little girl's mother – and leave them with her to care for them. He gave them no financial support and was not involved in their lives. The household was in abject poverty since the mother and grandmother did not have any work. To hear the girl tell the story, she appeared to consider this a perfectly normal living situation since it's all she's ever known.

Then there's the story of two sisters in the Indonesia program. Their family had been living on a remote island off the coast of Bali, where their parents were doing agricultural work. There are no schools on that island, so their mother took the girls to Bali to stay with an uncle, and they were enrolled in school. While they were living with their uncle, their father died, leaving their mother in a very difficult situation. At that point, their uncle asked the girls if they wanted to make a trip into the city. Of course, they did! Going to the city was fun, and they looked forward to having a good time there. But instead of taking them to the city for a fun outing, their uncle took them to the orphanage. He abandoned them there without telling them ahead of time what he had planned.

Then there's the story of three siblings – two boys and a girl – in Liberia who were living in impoverished conditions with their father. The father became sick during the Ebola epidemic in 2014 and was hospitalized. There were no other family members who could care for the siblings, so a neighbor, who worked for the children's home, brought them there to be cared for. In all the years since then, their father has only come to see them once. Nothing is known about any other family members –

including their mother – and no one else has ever come to visit them.

One of the little boys in the children's home in Tanzania was found buried alive shortly after being born. He was found by a shepherd who heard his faint cries. A woman also came along and helped the shepherd with him. The baby was taken to the hospital, where the woman went to see him. She tried to strangle him when she learned he was going to be sent to the children's home! This boy was eventually adopted by our partner in Tanzania and is a sweet, well-adjusted little boy despite his horrible start in life.

Then there's the story of one of the boys in the children's home in Eswatini. A news crew had gone to a neighborhood in the city to cover a story. While they were in that neighborhood, the people living there told the crew about a terrible situation with a little boy. The crew went to investigate and found the little boy - probably around two years old – locked in a shed by himself, without food and water. The neighbors said the woman they assumed was his mother was mentally ill and would leave him locked in there alone for days while she disappeared. The neighbors tried to help and would toss food to him through the windows. If the woman came back and caught them, she would get violent with them, so they were afraid to do much more. The crew was horrified by what they heard and notified the police, who came and broke down the door of the shed. They found the little boy in there, filthy, malnourished, and surviving by eating his own feces. The story was run on television that night and our partner, Thabsile, saw it on the news. She never imagined the boy would be brought to her children's home by the police just a few hours later. The police tried to find the woman who was assumed to be his mother, but she never returned. That little boy has thrived in the care of the children's home and has grown into a sweet, intelligent young man.

We interviewed one young woman in the Congo program just two weeks after her father had been killed. Rebels had come to their home and had found them hiding inside the house. They dragged her father outside and chopped him to death with a machete while the rest of the family looked on in horror.

In the Dominican program, we have had children who told us their mother "worked in a pool hall" or "sold rocks." We learned these are slang expressions for prostitution or selling drugs. It breaks our hearts to know these young children are aware of what their mothers are doing.

Frequently when we hear these kinds of stories, one of us on the team will end up sponsoring the child. It's a natural response to hearing something like this. On one trip, our Haitian translator, Danny, was translating for Philip while he interviewed a little girl. Danny had grown up in a children's home in Haiti himself. As he heard the answers this little girl gave to the questions Philip asked, he stopped, looked at Philip, and said, "That is my story. I would be in the same situation as her if I had not ended up in the children's home. I am going to sponsor her!"

As hard as it is to listen to the children's stories, we know it's important to have this information so we can search for a sponsor who can help. It was such an unexpected blessing to see Danny step out in faith and make the decision to sponsor this little girl because, if anyone could empathize with her situation, it was him.

One of the most encouraging interviews happened with a young girl in Kigali, Rwanda. Her parents had lived through the genocide and were doing their best to take care of their daughter, even though things were difficult for them. Joy was one of those students who shined when she came into the room. She always had a smile on her face and a charming personality. She truly lived up to the name her parents had given her. However, one of the most remarkable things about Joy is one of the letters she gave us for her sponsors when she was in the sixth grade. In it, she said, "I really have a lot to thank you for, but let me end up telling you that your support is the best thing that has ever happened in my life. As I grow up I won't disappoint you. I will keep making you proud. Also, one of my goals in life is to help people in need of something that I am capable of doing. That is why I hope that in my future I will have the ability of helping children, like me, who can make good grades in class but who have financial problems, as one of my ways of thanking you."

There you have it. Yes, it is sad. Yes, it is hard to hear some of these stories. As hard as it is to hear them, it's even harder for these children to live those stories. For them, they're not just stories. This is their life. God has called us to do what we can to try to help. We do the interviews, take the measurements and the photos, put the children's info on our website, speak to audiences when given an opportunity, and do the mundane tasks of keeping track of all this information to make the programs function. Ultimately, the best thing we can do is to pray. We promise all our partners we will do everything we can to find sponsors for the children, but we all know that our efforts can only do so much. We can't make someone decide to sponsor a child. Only God can do that. Only He can reach down into someone's heart and stir it to love and good works, deciding to reach out and sponsor a child. We encourage our partners, the children, and their parents, to pray along with us that God will stir up sponsors for the children. And we will continue to do so for as long as He allows.

"What good is it, my brothers and sisters, if someone claims to have faith but has no deeds? Can such faith save them? Suppose a brother or a sister is without clothes and daily food. If one of you says to them, 'Go in peace; keep warm and well fed,' but does nothing about their physical needs, what good is it? In the same way, faith by itself, if it is not accompanied by action, is dead." (James 2:14-17 NIV)

Interviewing a little girl with a difficult story in Haiti (photo courtesy of Steve Lamb)

12

HOW DO YOU CHOOSE

"How can you see all those children in need and not want to sponsor all of them? How do you ever choose one out of the multitudes?"

I want to sponsor all of them, but I am not the one who chooses. I know I am supposed to sponsor a particular child when God gives me His unmistakable nudge. I don't always know why "that one" is the one, but He does, and my responsibility is simply to obey.

A great example of this starts way back – long before the birth of His Hands Support Ministries. When I was in college, my roommate and I sponsored a little boy in Korea. It was kind of a neat thing to do, but we soon lost interest and let the sponsorship lapse. Several years later, Philip and I were married and had our first two children, Kirstin and Holly. We were living in Maine then, in a very remote area, so I listened to a Christian radio station throughout the day to have someone "keep us company."

On the Focus on the Family program one day, I heard about a relatively new organization called Friends of the Americas. Friends of the Americas was started by Louisiana

Representative Woody Jenkins and his wife, Diane. The purpose of the organization was to promote friendship and understanding between the people of the United States and the people of Honduras.

At that time, Honduras was experiencing a time of conflict with the Sandinistas rebelling in Central America, creating turbulent times. During the radio program, Friends asked people to fill shoeboxes of Christmas gifts that would be given to impoverished Honduran children. We thought it would be a good family project for our girls, so we decided to participate. This put us on their mailing list. Not long after, we received a newsletter saying Friends had decided to start a sponsorship program for the children they helped in a small community called Trojes in Honduras.

My previous experience of sponsoring a child in college came back to my mind, and I felt some sense of guilt over letting the sponsorship lapse, so Philip and I decided to take on a sponsorship with Friends. The year was 1986. We set the sponsorship up in the names of our daughters, and we were assigned a little three-year-old girl named Nolvia. It seemed like the perfect choice since Holly and Kirstin were ages two and four at the time. Kirstin thought of Nolvia as another little sister. We continued faithfully sponsoring Nolvia until she aged out of the program. We were then assigned a second child, Rebeca, who was about three years old.

Through all the years of our sponsorship, we regularly received newsletters telling us about the projects they were doing and describing the area of Trojes. We read each one, trying to imagine the things we were reading about, especially the description of a road from the city of Danli into Trojes, which Friends' workers had to travel regularly. The road had earned the title of "Most Dangerous Road in the Americas" because the Sandinistas would lie in wait in a mountain just across the border into Nicaragua. The mountain was on the other side of a valley beside the road, and the Sandinistas would pick off vehicles driving along the road like ducks in a shooting gallery. For me, reading these descriptions was like trying to imagine the planet Mars. The idea that I might one day see these places in person was unimaginable.

A number of years after our sponsorship started, we received a letter from Friends talking about a new clinic they were building somewhere. In that letter, they said a plaque would be put on the wall in this new clinic. The plaque would have the names of the original sponsors on it as a way to honor the sponsors who had been with them from the beginning. I remember reading that to Kirstin and Holly and telling them that somewhere, in the middle of nowhere, in the far-away country of Honduras, there was a plaque on a clinic wall with their names on it. Maybe, one day, they might actually be able to see it in person, even though none of us could really imagine that ever happening. It was like telling them that they might go to Mars one day.

As the years went by, and we continued receiving newsletters from Friends each month, God began to use Philip and me to begin His Hands Support Ministries. His Hands then began to branch out into many different countries, including Honduras. During one of our visits there, we talked to our primary partner, Pastor Julio Pavon, and asked him if he had ever heard of Friends of the Americas. He hadn't heard of them, but when we started talking to him about the city of Danli and the community of Trojes, he did know of those places. In fact, back in the 1980s, when the hostilities with the Sandinistas were ongoing, Pastor Julio, who was an officer in the Honduran army at that time, had been stationed in Trojes! We asked him if he would be willing to go with us if we were able to contact Friends of the Americas and set up a time for us to visit there. He was thrilled with the idea and agreed to do whatever he could to facilitate a visit.

Once we were back in the U.S., I contacted the offices of Friends in Louisiana, explained who we were, and asked if we could arrange to visit the work in Trojes. I also mentioned the plaque we had read about so many years earlier and asked if anyone knew where the clinic was where the plaque had been placed. The lovely woman I spoke to on the phone didn't know what I was talking about: it had been too many years since that letter had been sent out, and she knew nothing about it. They were happy to arrange for us to visit Trojes, but I gave up on the idea of seeing that plaque.

Later on, I went out on a limb and sent an email to Friends asking if it would be possible to visit our sponsored child, Rebeca. I also asked if it was at all possible to meet Nolvia, if she was still in the area and if anyone knew where she was. Even though we never received an answer to that email about meeting the girls, we were determined to go to Trojes anyway since Pastor Julio was willing to accompany us and Friends was willing to arrange for us to visit. In July of 2014, we found ourselves on a flight into Tegucigalpa, the capital of Honduras, where Pastor Julio lives.

Flying into Tegucigalpa was one of the items on our imaginary bucket list because we had heard stories and seen videos of just how challenging it is to land a jet there. And they were right! Pastor Julio met us at the airport and brought us to his home, where we prepared to go out to Trojes the next day. The plan was to go to Danli first and have lunch at the home of Dr. Hector Zepeda, the doctor who oversees the Friends' clinic. Then Dr. Zepeda would accompany us out to Trojes and show us around.

On July 19, 2014, we found ourselves in the home of Dr. Zepeda, meeting the man we had read about in so many newsletters from Friends and hearing first hand from him about the work going on in Trojes. Imagine our surprise when, in the course of the conversation, Pastor Julio mentioned that he had been stationed in Trojes back in the 1980s, and Dr. Zepeda said his father had also been stationed there! They compared notes and discovered that Pastor Julio knew Dr. Zepeda's father as they had been stationed there at the same time! There are no coincidences in God's plan!

Once our lunch was finished, we loaded into a vehicle and started the drive to Trojes. Suddenly all those things we had read about in the newsletters became real to us. The scenery was just as we had imagined it. Then we found ourselves on that stretch of road we had heard about so many times – what used to be known as The Most Dangerous Road in the Americas – and now we understood what they meant when they said it was like a shooting gallery. There was a valley on the right-hand side of the narrow road, and just across the valley was the border of Nicaragua. My phone even sent me a "Welcome to Nicaragua" text as the cell signal began bouncing off towers across the border. On the left-hand side of the road, there was a hill going straight up from the roadside. Any vehicle traveling this stretch would be exposed to snipers across that valley and could be picked off as easily as ducks in a shooting gallery. We were thankful those hostilities had come to an end as we continued on our way to Trojes.

When we arrived at Friends' clinic, it was just as emotional as when we crossed the border into Rwanda that first time. Visiting here was something we had only dreamed about and never imagined we would ever be able to do. With a huge smile on my face, I got out of the vehicle and started walking into the building. As we walked towards the door, we passed a young woman sitting on a bench on the sidewalk. I noticed her, but it wasn't until we had passed by her that I thought, *That looks like Nolvia!* I couldn't believe it would actually be her or that I would recognize her. She would be thirty years old by now, and the last photo we had seen of her was more than thirteen years before. So, I told myself not to be foolish and kept walking into the building.

Once we entered a large waiting area, I saw another young woman. It was Rebeca! I had no doubt it was her, even though it had been a few years since we had seen her photo. She was standing right in front of us, with the sweetest smile on her face. I just started crying and gave her a huge hug.

While we were still hugging, Dr. Zepeda interrupted us and asked me if I had seen Nolvia sitting on the bench outside!! *It was her*!! I turned around, and she was standing right beside me! I started sobbing at that point and grabbed her into a huge hug. I couldn't believe they had kept track of her and knew how to find her so we could meet her for the very first time.

There is no way to describe all the emotions we had at that meeting. We had no idea we would meet either girl. I couldn't let myself hope we would - especially Nolvia - since it had been so long since our sponsorship had ended. But, the people at Friends had contacted her and Rebeca and had them both waiting there to meet us.

We all tried to get our emotions under control and sat down on a bench in the waiting area. We began getting to know one another better, reveling in the fact that God had allowed this unimaginable meeting to take place. But God wasn't done yet. As I looked up to speak to Dr. Zepeda, who was standing in front of us, I glanced up over his head to some frames on the wall behind him. It was hard to see it well from where I was sitting, but then some of the wording came into focus, and I gasped. Dr. Zepeda seemed puzzled by my reaction and started to look around to see what was causing it. I almost shouted when I asked him, *"Is that the plaque??!!"* There it was – right there on the wall of a clinic out in the middle of nowhere in Honduras – a plaque with the names Kirstin and Holly Charles on it, and I broke down sobbing.

There are no words to describe how it felt to see all that God had done from way back in 1986, when we started our sponsorships with Friends, until that day in 2014. We tried to explain it all to Dr. Zepeda, and he had tears in his eyes as he said, "God is doing something here today..." Yes, Dr. Zepeda, He was. And He still is.

That day will be with me forever, and I think of it often. Rebeca has now aged out of the program herself, so Friends has assigned another little girl to us named Loheidy. I hope to someday return to Trojes and meet her too.

But to get back to the question at the start of this chapter, sometimes God's nudge to sponsor a particular child comes with a backstory. Because in January of 2018, when I was on one of our teams in the community of Teotecacinte in Nicaragua, our Nicaraguan friends told us we were very close to the border of Honduras. I asked them if they knew of a place in Honduras called Trojes, and they looked shocked. "How do you know Trojes?!" they asked me. I explained about our connection to Friends of the Americas and our visit to Trojes just three and a half years earlier. Then they told me there was a border crossing just three kilometers from where we were sitting, and Trojes was on the other side of that crossing! Are you serious?! It was just three kilometers away!

Then God did what He loves to do and gave me a little nudge in the form of a sweet young girl who approached our interview table to be put into the sponsorship program. When we asked her name, I heard her say the same name – both the first name and the last name – as "our" Rebeca in Trojes. And I smiled and said, "Yes, God. We will sponsor this new Rebeca."

"Trust in the Lord with all your heart, and lean not on your own understanding; in all your ways acknowledge Him, and He shall direct your paths." (Proverbs 3:5-6 NKJV)

(Left to Right) Philip, Rebeca, Nolvia, and me

13

UNEXPECTED BLESSINGS

"It sounds as though you've placed yourselves on the pathway to blessing."

We may be on that pathway, but it is God who has placed us there. We love it when He gives us unexpected and unanticipated blessings while walking the path He has set for us. Blessings like having a merchant in a craft market in Kampala, Uganda, stop and pray over us when she learned we would soon be traveling back to the U.S. It didn't matter to her that we had not purchased anything from her. She was our sister in Christ and, even though we had just met, she did what sisters do. She stopped and prayed over us.

Our partners in Mexico, Franco Mendez and his wife, Barby, were sent out as missionaries from their home church in Puebla, Mexico, to the small mountain community of Cuautotola several hours away. The community is a very closed community where outsiders are not readily accepted. Initially, it was difficult for Franco and Barby to reach out to those in the community who were wary of outsiders. Despite this, they were able to establish their ministry, and it was growing by the time we formed our partnership with them. The people, who are mostly Catholic, were amazed when they realized a program being run through an evangelical church would support children from Catholic families. Through this, the sponsorship program has positively impacted Franco's church by giving it a good name in the community. These results are not things we anticipated when we began our partnership with Franco and Barby, but it is an unexpected and much-appreciated blessing that has come out of it. Franco feels that families who are part of the program are also very appreciative.

On one of our Honduras trips, college student Beth wanted to receive college credit for the trip towards her criminal justice major. Before the trip, she and her professor created a list of questions for Beth to ask. She sent the questions to the Honduras coordinator, who sent them to the lead pastor, Pastor Julio. He responded, saying Beth absolutely could *not* ask any of the questions as it could put the people in danger. She understood and accepted his response.

Then on the trip one day, when the team was on their way to a church to work, the team's two vehicles drove up beside a vehicle with police in it. Team member, Wanda, waved to the police, who waved back at her, as did the team members sitting in the other vehicle. The police were curious about why several Americans were in their country, so they followed the team to the church.

The pastor at the church shared with the police for quite a while and invited them to lunch – an invitation the police accepted. Wanda told Beth God had placed these police there for her to talk to, so Beth sat down with them while they ate. She told them she was studying criminal justice in college, and they told her about their jobs.

Throughout the conversation, the police answered all of Beth's questions without her ever asking any of them.

The pastor shared the gospel message with the police, and the team was able to pray with them. Beth did not expect she would be able to get the answers to the questions her college professor wanted her to ask. No one anticipated they would be feeding police that day – not only with physical food but also with spiritual food. But God...

In December of 2009, we took a team to Guatemala. Long-time ministry volunteer and board member Jamie Dennett was a member of that team. Our hosts at the mission house – Carlos and Heidi Fernandez – invited us to go to a Christmas program one evening. It was held at the school their children attended, which is a school for missionary children, so the program was mostly in English. We had an enjoyable time watching the performances. As we sat in the audience, Jamie Dennett was looking through the program and reading the names of the children who were performing. She noticed a couple of the children had the last name Dennett, which is not a particularly common family name. After the program ended, she talked to Heidi about the children with the last name of Dennett and discovered they were very good friends of Heidi's children. Their parents were also at the Christmas program, so Heidi found them and introduced them to Jamie D. Their names were Brian and Mary Dennett. In comparing notes, Jamie D discovered that Brian and Mary were also from Maine! She questioned them about their family connections – parents, grandparents, aunts, uncles, and cousins – and mentioned that her husband's name is Scott Dennett. During their conversation, Jamie D discovered Brian was the son of one of Scott's first cousins! Jamie D had never met Brian or Mary before and had no idea there were any

Christians in that portion of the family, but here were Brian and Mary, who were missionaries in Guatemala! It was an unexpected blessing to discover not only this family connection but also a common bond in Jesus Christ! They have remained in communication and have continued to build on their new-found relationship.

By the fall of 2007, we had added several more communities to our Haiti program. To see all the children we needed to see, we decided to split up our twelve-member team into two groups and send the groups out to two different communities on the same day. This was the first time we ever did that, and it went well.

Matt led the group that went out to Danda. In his group were team members, Laura, a physician's assistant, and Mary, a nurse. Laura and Mary handled the children's photos that day, which turned out to be a decision with far-reaching implications. As one little girl came through to be photographed, Laura picked her up to set her down on the chair they were using. When she lifted her, she couldn't help but notice the little girl's stomach was distended and very hard. Both she and Mary observed the little girl didn't sit straight on the chair but leaned to one side as though she was in discomfort. They made a mental note about it but had to keep moving as children kept coming through. In hindsight, we wonder if someone without medical training would have even picked up on these subtle clues that something was wrong.

A bit later, Laura and Mary became aware that this same little girl had apparently had a bathroom accident. They took her over to the clinic next to the church building (a clinic run by the church in Danda) to clean her up, which was another thing someone without medical training might not have volunteered to do. As they cleaned her up, they were horrified to discover she did not have an anus. She was approximately seven or eight years old at the time, and it was unimaginable to both Laura and Mary that this girl had lived to this age without having the situation addressed. Her accident was the only way feces could be eliminated from her body, and it was coming out from areas where feces should never be. Her body had obviously created a fistula to eliminate feces, but the girl had no control over it.

Laura and Mary asked to see her interview form to see how her health question had been answered, and it said she was in good health. Apparently, when she was interviewed, no one had told us about her problem because they assumed nothing could be done about it. As the team was leaving Danda to go back to the mission house, they saw this same little girl – whose name is Rose – walking along the road. They picked her up and gave her a ride home, all the while wondering what on earth could be done to help her.

As soon as the two groups got back together at the mission house, Laura and Mary told me about what they had discovered, and we started to discuss what to do. The only obvious answer was to talk to Pastor Elima (the pastor in Danda) and ask him how we could help.

At that time, an American missionary doctor visited the clinic in Danda regularly and Pastor Elima consulted him about Rose and her condition. It was clear she needed corrective surgery, but before it could happen, she needed to have a colostomy so the feces could exit her body without continually contaminating other areas and to eliminate the pressure inside her abdomen. All of this would be costly, but we began to raise money to help make it possible.

Eventually, she had her colostomy surgery, and in the process, they discovered a huge mass of calcified feces that never would have cleared her system. If something had not been done soon, this situation could have proved deadly. The mass was successfully removed, the colostomy performed, and Rose's life and health began to improve immediately.

In order to completely remedy her situation, she was going to need corrective surgery that would best be performed across the border in the Dominican Republic. This would involve getting Rose a passport and then finding someone to care for her over in the Dominican. Like many developing countries, when someone goes into the hospital, they need someone with them to take care of their personal needs like bathing them, getting food for them, feeding them, and getting prescribed medicines so the doctors and nurses can administer them. All this would be expensive.

Again, funds were raised, Pastor Elima was able to obtain a passport for her, and Rose went to the Dominican and had the surgery she needed. She had to spend some time there for her recovery, but once she was completely healed, she returned to Haiti, and her life was completely changed. She had full function and control and led a normal life. This took many years to accomplish and a lot of effort on the part of many, many people. But it was worth it in the end when we saw Rose flourishing. She wants to be a nurse, and anything is possible for her now.

When God sent us to partner with Franco and Barby, we never expected our partnership to have such a positive impact on how the community viewed his ministry. When God sent our team to Honduras, we never expected that visit to result in Honduran policemen being fed - not only physical food but spiritual food as well. When God sent Jamie D to Guatemala in 2009, she never expected to meet a cousin who was a missionary and a believer in Jesus Christ. When our team went to Danda that day back in

2007, they never anticipated becoming involved in helping to save a young girl's life. We don't always anticipate these kinds of things, but we know God is busy weaving an intricate tapestry. From our perspective, at the back side of His tapestry, it just looks like a mess of unrelated threads. But when He finally shows us the front side of His tapestry, we will be amazed to see how all the threads come together to make an incredibly beautiful picture. But God...

"Oh, the depth of the riches both of the wisdom and knowledge of God! How unsearchable are His judgments and His ways past finding out!" (Romans 11:33 NIV)

Wanda enjoying the unexpected blessing of visiting a school in India

14

IT'S ABOUT SHOWING UP

"What do you do when you make these trips to visit your partners?"

Our primary objective is always to gather information on all the children and adults in the programs. In some cases, this information is updated information from a previous trip that will either go to a sponsor (if the child or adult has a sponsor) or will be used to create an information sheet for a sponsor once the child or adult is chosen. Sometimes our partners ask us to add new children and adults to the programs, so we need to get information on them too. This is a way of providing accountability to the sponsors. We see each child and adult in the programs, verify they're still participating, and verify they are receiving the things they are supposed to receive as a result of being sponsored. Even though that's always our primary objective, it's not always the only thing we do when we're there.

There are times when our partners have asked us to get involved in other projects in their ministry. We have helped with construction projects and feeding programs, played with children, had special times with tea and crafts with the mothers of the children in the program, done in-home visits, and various other things as we have been asked to help.

But sometimes, it's just about showing up – being there with our partners and investing ourselves in their ministry and in their lives. It's also about showing up and having fellowship with the people involved in our partners' ministries. Like the time Pastor Noël in Haiti took our small team to the tiny, remote village of Ouvray for the first time.

There were just three of us on the team – board member Bea, daughter Holly, and me. We showed up in the middle of their church service, which Pastor Noël interrupted with our arrival. He had us go up to the front of their makeshift shelter where they met for their service and sit up in front of everyone. If that wasn't uncomfortable enough, he told them I would get up and greet them! This was early on in our ministry in Haiti, and I could only speak what I refer to as "survival Creole" at the time. I was horrified when I realized he was gesturing at me to come up there to stand by him and greet everyone. But I did what he asked, walked up there, and started to speak to them in their heart language of Creole. At the end of every phrase and sentence I spoke, everyone gathered there shouted at the top of their lungs, *"Amen!!!"* Some even stood on their feet and shouted, *"Amen!!!"* After a few feeble sentences, I went and sat back down with Holly and Bea. They leaned over and whispered to me, telling me they were amazed at the congregation's reaction, and asked me what on earth I had said. This is what I said that day: "Hello! We are so happy to see you today! We have many friends in the United States and they are praying for you!" And that's it. We were all shocked by their reaction until we talked to Pastor Noël later, and he told us we were the first white missionaries who had ever visited Ouvray. It wasn't about what I said. It was the fact that we showed up and the fact that I made my feeble attempt to speak to them in their heart language. It was a blessing to all of us that day.

During the first few years of our ministry in Haiti, we would notice Pastor Noël's wife, Marie, would start to get quiet and look sad a day or two before we had to leave. We knew she was anticipating our departure and didn't want to see us go, but we were always touched by how sad she seemed to get. She would always ask us, "Are you coming back?" when we would leave, and we had to reassure her that we would certainly be back.

Then one day, she sat us down and told us a parable. She started by saying we had probably noticed how sad she got in the days leading up to our departure day. Then she said this: "When you come, it's like when someone is preparing to have a baby. There's a lot of preparation that has to happen and a lot of tiring work, but everyone does it with joy because they know the baby is coming. When the baby arrives, it is a lot more work with so many things to do, but, again, everyone does it with joy because the baby is here, even though it is very tiring. And then the baby dies... It's like that for us when you leave."

Another example was when we made our first trip to India. Nancy Millar had asked us to visit one of the ministries she was still trying to help on her own because, at that time, she had never been able to visit them in person. We had no idea what we were committing to, but we agreed to make the ten-hour overnight journey by train to visit the Anamani Home for her.

When we arrived at the home, they had decorated the entire courtyard with flower petals and beautiful chalk art on the ground. As we entered the gate, they tossed flower petals over all of us and then escorted us into their humble home. After some time for us to rest, they brought us into a room with three folding chairs in it and asked Philip, Pastor Michael, and me to sit in the chairs. Then they brought each of us a plate of food to eat, holding the plates on our laps, while the entire household of over twenty adults and children stood around the perimeter of the room watching us. In India, the custom is to eat with your right hand - without utensils - but apparently, our hosts at the Anamani Home had done their homework because they proudly walked up to Philip and me and held out a couple of forks, wrapped in a napkin like prized possessions, and said, "We bought you these!"

But the most meaningful point of the day happened later, when we were walking with the Anamani Home leaders, Durga and Sujeeth. While we were walking, Sujeeth said he was of the Dalit caste and was, therefore, untouchable. When Philip heard this, he put his arm around Sujeeth's shoulders, gave him a big hug, and said, "You are *not* untouchable. You are my brother."

On our first visit to Cuba with Leticia and the Bells, we were asked to visit a pastor in an area of Cuba that is known for spirit worship. It's a difficult place for Pastor Santos[1] to serve, but he knows this is where God would have him. The denomination in which he serves is only allowed to have house churches in Cuba, and, by definition, a house church can only have 30 people who attend. Because of this regulation, Pastor Santos has had his church shut down by the government seven times, confiscating his building each time. Since it's a house church, this means he not only lost his church; he also lost his house. Yet, he still continues in the good works God has given him to do even though the discouragement is real and he has had a difficult time.

It was in this context that we made our first visit. He was so happy to see us and shocked that we would bother to come and meet him and learn about his ministry. Before we left, we all gave him a bit of money to help him continue working on the projects he had. We promised him we would return, but I don't think he believed us. Because when he saw us entering his church just a few months later, tears started streaming down his face. He couldn't believe we really did come back. Sometimes it's about just showing up...

What a blessing it is whenever we visit the homes of the elderly people in the feeding program in Honduras. Most times, we are greeted with exclamations of thankfulness and praise to God that we have come to visit them. It's beautiful and humbling at the same time.

In Kenya, when the team visited the home of a woman with leprosy, Bishop Ogol's wife, Everlyn, apologized to the team for the smell. When Marilee asked, "What smell?" Everlyn responded with tears saying the team had truly been sent by God. It was another humbling experience.

Then there was my first meeting with Thabsile Thwala in Eswatini. During that first visit, I was there for a meeting of their board of directors for The Fortress. As I mentioned in a previous chapter, The Fortress had previously been supported by another ministry, but when the leadership in that ministry changed, their relationship with The Fortress had ended. The new leadership had asked Thabsile and their board to make changes with which they were not comfortable. Even though they knew it meant they would lose their support, they felt they had no choice and decided to simply trust God and not make those changes. It was during this time Barb Halvorson had asked us to partner with The Fortress, which we did, even though we hadn't made a visit there ourselves and wouldn't be able to go there for another year.

When I was finally meeting their board for the first time, I had two separate conversations that cemented in our minds that this was a God-ordained partnership. One of their board members approached me during a time of fellowship after the meeting and said, "We are so thankful for your willingness to partner with us. If you had not stepped in to help, we would have been forced to close the children's home. We see that as a miracle of God, and we thank Him for it." Praise God! Exactly the response we would hope for – praising God and not us! But then the icing on the cake came later. After the fellowship time was over, Thabsile took me into her office so we could spend some one-on-one time getting to know one another better. In our conversation, she said this: "We are so thankful for your willingness to partner with us. If you had not stepped in to help, we would have been forced to close the children's home. We see that as a miracle of God, and we thank Him for it." It was exactly the same thing the board member had said to me during the time of fellowship!! I saw this as another miracle of God!

Our ultimate goal in everything we do is to have it result in praise to God and not to us. *"This service that you perform is not only supplying the needs of the Lord's people but is also overflowing in many expressions of thanks to God."* 2 Corinthians 9:12 NIV. He is the focus of everything we do, and we don't want any praise to be deflected to us. It takes effort to turn the spotlight on God instead of on us: the rich, white Americans who came to visit.

We also have to remind ourselves that the good works God has prepared for us to do today may look very different from what we expect. It could be something as simple as making a stumbling effort to speak to someone in their heart language. Or it could be showing up at the church of a very discouraged pastor or the home of a lonely elderly person. Or it could be putting your arm around a brother who thinks he is untouchable. It could be something as simple as having a willing spirit to do whatever it is God puts in front of you to do. We just have to keep our eyes on Him, and He will direct us to the things He has for us to do each day: whether it's in a foreign country or at home.

"Therefore if there is any consolation in Christ, if any comfort of love, if any fellowship of the Spirit, if any affection and mercy, fulfill my joy by being like-minded, having the same love, being of one accord, of one mind." (Philippians 2:1-2 NKJV)

Honduras coordinator, Lori, praying with one of the senior ladies in the Honduras program

15

LISTEN TO OUR HOSTS

"Doesn't it make you uncomfortable going to strange places, working with people who do things in strange ways? I wouldn't know what to do..."

"When God asks us to do something uncomfortable, it's usually because He wants to do something remarkable." - Charles Stanley.[1]

One of our main guiding principles when visiting our partners is listening to our hosts. If they tell us we shouldn't do a particular thing, we don't do it. If they tell us we should do a particular thing, we do it. In both cases, we can often be uncomfortable with this principle. Yet we realize it's important to stick to it because our hosts know, better than we do, the right and wrong way to do things in their country. Beyond that, our hosts know - probably better than we do - how to trust God and walk by faith. We try very hard to follow that example.

When we started the sponsorship program in Haiti, we were only helping Pastor Noël in Terrier Rouge. Before too long, he asked us to go out to the small village of Paulette to help the pastor there with the children in his school. Then he said something we've never forgotten. "They are very poor out there." Looking around Terrier Rouge, we would have said the people there were very poor, and most of them are. Then to hear Pastor Noël ask us to go out to another community and help them too, because "they are very poor out there" was powerful and humbling. Of course, we did what he asked. As of this writing, he has sent us out to many more communities in Northeast Haiti, all because of his love for his people and his love for his Savior. We have done what he has asked every time.

In Eswatini, we stay on the grounds of a small Bible school. They have little guest cottages, and for a small fee, they allow guests to use them. It's a lovely place, but we listened to our partner very carefully when she told us to watch out for the small holes in the ground between where our vehicle was parked and the front door of our cottage. She told us those holes were snake holes, and mambas and cobras were living in them. From that point on, we were *very* careful about where we stepped, especially after some kids staying in an adjacent cottage excitedly told us their family had killed three cobras and a mamba on the lawn while we were gone for the day! There was also a large dog that came and slept on our porch at night, right up against the door. We had no idea who the dog belonged to or why he was there, but I like to think he was keeping the snakes away from our door.

In Cuba, we must be extremely careful about what we say and what we do. Our friends there have told us that someone is always listening and someone is always watching. There are spies everywhere, but no one knows who they might be. While we are not overly concerned about our own welfare, we do not want to cause any problems for our friends, so we guard our mouths very carefully.

On our first visit to India, when we went to see the Anamani Home for Nancy, Pastor Michael arranged for us to go there on an overnight train. He had booked confirmed tickets for the three of us but apparently *confirmed* doesn't necessarily mean you have a confirmed spot on the train. The car we were in was a sleeper car, and each compartment will hold six people. When the conductor saw our tickets, he told Pastor Michael we did not have a confirmed compartment. We had to look around and find an empty spot. The only trouble with this plan was when other people would get on the train at various stops and find us in their confirmed compartment.

During the ten-hour overnight trip, we moved seven times. We knew we had hit an all-time low when we found ourselves sitting on the floor at the end of the train car outside the bathrooms. If you know anything at all about the type of facilities they have in India (squatty potties on the floor), you'll understand that the floor of the bathroom and, subsequently, the floor around the area of the bathroom gets pretty wet.

After we visited the Anamani Home, we had to go back to the train that evening and repeat the ten-hour trip back. This time we at least had tickets with a confirmed compartment. We spent some time sitting with the other three people in our compartment – all men – before it was time to go to sleep. This is an interesting process because the compartment seats are similar to bus seats that face one another with a table you pull down between them if you need it. However, when you want to go to sleep, everyone in the compartment has to agree to go to bed at the same time because there are six berths - three on each side, stacked one over the other. The bottom berths on each side are the seats the passengers sit on, facing one another. The other four are stacked above those bottom ones – two on each side - with not enough space to sit up once you're on them. So once those upper berths are folded down, everyone has to lie down on their own berth.

Being the only woman in our compartment, I had little influence concerning who would sleep on each berth, so the men assigned me the middle berth on one side. Pastor Michael was on the berth under mine, and Philip was on the berth over me. This meant I was lying on a berth, looking across a *very* narrow space at a man I didn't know, sleeping directly across from me. When I had to get up to use the bathroom, I had to climb down onto Pastor Michael's berth and sit down beside him to put my shoes on. This still ranks as my all-time-most-uncomfortable travel experience – especially since by the time we arrived back in Pastor Michael's city, I was starting to exhibit the symptoms of chikungunya (more on this later). However, the remarkable visit to the Anamani Home made it all worth it.

One example of a rare occasion when we *didn't* listen to our host was when Marilee and I went into the Dominican Republic from Haiti with Pastor Elima. We were going there to visit Rose – the young girl from Danda who needed medical intervention. She had gone there for surgery and was recovering where she could be close to the hospital and her doctor. She was staying with a woman who had agreed to care for her. It was difficult for Rose to be away from home in a country where the heart language of Spanish is not the same as her Creole while trying to recover from all the medical interventions which had been done to her.

We were happy to go and visit her to try and cheer her up and bring her a gift from her sponsor. But once we crossed the border at Dajabon and were waiting in the small bus to take us to the city of Santiago where Rose was staying, I noticed the clock at the front of the bus. We had lost an hour just crossing the border since the Dominican is in a time zone one hour ahead of Haiti. Doing the calculations based on the time I saw on that clock and, realizing the journey to Santiago would take three hours one way, I came to the conclusion there was no way we would get back to the border before it closed for the night. When I mentioned my concern to Pastor Elima, he looked up at the clock, thought about it for about half a second, and then said, "Eh – we'll try!" So, off we went.

Along the way, the bus was stopped at random intervals by men with big guns. They would get on the bus and start randomly asking to see people's papers. They were selective about who they asked, and Marilee and I couldn't figure out their criteria. We were praying they wouldn't take an interest in the only two women on the bus who had light skin. At one of those stops, they threw a young man off the bus because they didn't like the look of his papers. He was telling them he was a student and had exactly the documentation he needed, but they didn't listen and threw him off anyway – in a remote area surrounded by cane fields. We had no idea who they were or why they were doing that, but we were very happy they didn't choose to throw Marilee and me off the bus in the middle of nowhere!

Eventually, the bus arrived in Santiago, and when we got off, we realized Pastor Elima didn't know where to go. He had a small scrap of paper in his hand with the address written on it, but he didn't know where the address was located. He also couldn't speak Spanish, so we had no idea how we were going to find that address. Pastor Elima stopped a young man on the street, showed him the piece of paper, and the young man gestured that the address was just up the street a couple of blocks from where we stood! Talk about walking by faith!

We followed the young man's directions and found Rose, looking happy and healthy, and had a great visit with her. Pastor Elima still didn't seem concerned about the time, but once we got back on another bus and started to head back to the border, I looked at the clock and realized there was no way we would make it in time. The border was due to close in one hour, and we had just left Santiago. I began to send text messages to the rest of the people on our team, who were still in Haiti, asking them to ask Marie what we should do. She talked with Pastor Noël and then sent back a message saying it was our decision. Marilee and I had no idea what we should do. We were not able to talk to Pastor Elima about it until we arrived in Dajabon because the bus was very crowded, and we were not seated near one another.

When we arrived in Dajabon and got off the bus, Pastor Elima started to make a beeline for the border, which had closed two hours earlier. I stopped him and asked him what we were going to do because the border was closed. He said it would be okay because we could cross through the water. (The border crossing in that part of the country crosses a shallow river. There is a bridge over it, but once the border closes for the day, the bridge is closed.) Right then, I broke our own rule and said we couldn't do that. He didn't understand and asked me if we were afraid to go through the water. I responded by telling him we couldn't do that because it was illegal. He countered by telling me there were police at the border and we could give them some money, and they'd let us cross through the water. "But no, Pas! We can't do that. If we cross through the water when the border is closed, there won't be anyone on the other side to stamp our passports back into the country or give us a green card! Then when we have to leave Haiti to go home, we won't have an entry stamp in our passport, and we won't have a green card!" (Tourists are given a green immigration card when they enter Haiti, which they must turn back in when they exit the country.)

He thought about it for a second and then realized we were right. We couldn't cross into Haiti that way without being in a world of trouble later. This thought had never occurred to him because it's not a serious issue for a Haitian to cross that way. Happens all the time. He had not thought about the implications it might have for an American.

We started looking around for a hotel. There was one just up the street from the bus station. It was upstairs – over a bar/pharmacy. And yes, it was just as sketchy as it sounds. Pastor Elima got us checked in and then left us there, saying he would come back for us in the morning. Marilee and I shoved a chair underneath the door handle in our room and slept on the top of the sheets rather than getting in. No telling what might have been in there.

We had nothing to eat and nothing to drink, so I got brave and went downstairs to the bar and, in my survival Spanish, asked for two bottles of cold water. We had no pesos to pay for the water, but they were kind and gave them to us anyway. Then Marilee and I split the eight pretzel sticks I had in my bag. Four pretzel sticks and a bottle of water had to serve as our lunch and dinner because we hadn't eaten anything since leaving the mission house that morning.

The next morning, we went downstairs to wait for Pastor Elima. While we were waiting, a woman came out of the bar and handed me a phone. I had no idea how she knew it was for me since she only spoke Spanish and Pastor Elima doesn't speak it at all, but it was him on the phone asking if we could find our own way back to the border. He had crossed through the river the night before, and if he had to cross back into the Dominican to get us, he would have to pay a fee to exit Haiti, another fee to enter the Dominican, and then two more fees to exit the Dominican and enter Haiti again. We had no idea how to get there on foot, so he told us to get a cab and he would meet us on the other side. No problem. But when I handed the phone back to the woman and said "Taxi??" she shook her head and said "Motoconcho." For those who might not know what that is, it's a motorcycle taxi. I can tell you it was quite a sight to see Marilee and me riding on the back of two separate motoconchos with Dominican men driving us to the border.

Eventually, we got back to Terrier Rouge, and the first thing Marie said to me was this – "Pastor Noël said he would be very angry if you crossed through the river." Yes! He told us to make the decision, and we made the right one!

For most of that journey to the Dominican, we were very uncomfortable doing things outside of our comfort zone. Even Pastor Elima was challenged with having to function outside of his comfort zone: having to deal with a language barrier and practices that have different implications for Haitians than they do for Americans. However, there were many remarkable outcomes; we got to spend time with Rose, showing her the love of Christ and cheering her up. We made it to Santiago and back – with a slight overnight delay – but survived the journey. We were given a chance to make our own decision about what to do, and we chose the right thing. God's mercy and grace were very evident throughout the whole journey, including the outcome.

God frequently challenges us to do uncomfortable things. Instead of facing these situations with fear or dread, we should view them with a sense of excitement, anticipating what remarkable thing God plans to bring out of our discomfort. I believe God gives us these kinds of challenges to strengthen our faith, bringing us closer to maturity. When we listen to God's leading and listen to our hosts, we can be confident of the outcome, and our faith will grow.

"Join together in following my example, brothers and sisters, and just as you have us as a model, keep your eyes on those who live as we do." (Philippians 3:17 NIV)

Sharing cramped quarters with Philip on an Indian train (notice my feet in the lower left corner of the photo)

16

GOD ANSWERS PRAYER

"You must be so brave to do the things you do."

My response to that statement is simple – "Not really." I believe that for someone to be brave, they must first be afraid of something; because it's in facing your fear that one becomes brave.

There have honestly been very few times in all our years of ministry when I have genuinely been afraid of something but had to do it anyway. I believe that lack of fear is only because there is peace and security in knowing you are doing exactly what God would have you do. To quote Tony Evans, "Faith does not automatically remove fear. It overrides it."[1] Does that mean fear never creeps in? Not at all. The enemy loves to use fear to try to distract us from the path God has traveling. One of the best ways to combat that fear is by keeping our eyes on the path and not on the things around the path that could stir up a spirit of fear.

One of those times I let fear creep in was when I had a minor panic attack on the sidewalk at Logan Airport in Boston when I had to lead a team on my own for the first time. It was September of 2004, and we were preparing for another return trip to Haiti. We were given an opportunity to give a presentation about our up-coming trip at New Hope Evangelical Free, which was the home church of one of our board members, Kathy Farmer. While we were there that Sunday, we learned the church was asking people to sign up to pray for our team in one-hour shifts, twenty-four hours a day, for the duration of our trip. I was overwhelmed that they would be willing to do this, and all the shifts quickly filled up – even those during the middle of the night. I would learn later just how vital this prayer would be to our team of five – all ladies.

This trip was the first trip I would lead without Philip, and I was scared. I had never considered taking a team to Haiti without him, and I had no idea how I could do it. However, it wasn't me who was doing it. It was God, and I just needed to depend on Him. I had asked Kathy, who was also going on the trip, to help me with some of the leadership responsibilities, which she agreed to do. We headed off to the airport, ready to walk in the good works again.

However, when it came time for me to say good-bye to Philip on the sidewalk at Logan Airport, I had a minor panic attack. You see, we knew that Tropical Storm Jeanne – which would soon become Hurricane Jeanne – was swirling around in the Caribbean, and we would likely cross paths with her in Haiti. Just the thought of facing Jeanne while I was responsible for this team of five ladies – including our daughter Kirstin again – had me petrified. I hung onto Philip telling him over and over that I couldn't do it; I couldn't take this team without him. He calmly reassured me I *could* do it and God would be with us the whole way and through the entire thing. It would have been very difficult for me to be obedient to the call to *go* in the future if I had given in and not gone, so I am thankful for Philip driving the enemy away with his words of encouragement. If I had given in to that fear, the enemy would have won a huge battle. I reluctantly turned and walked into the airport, dreading what was waiting for us.

The next morning, as we sat in the private terminal used by Missionary Flights International (MFI) in West Palm Beach, Florida, looking out the window at the destruction caused in West Palm by Hurricane Frances just a week before, we turned our eyes to the weather forecast on the television. At that exact moment, Hurricane Ivan was hitting the Florida panhandle. Then the forecaster showed us a radar image of Tropical Storm Jeanne and her projected path across the island of Puerto Rico, and then on to the north coast of the Dominican Republic and over Haiti's north coast – exactly where we were headed. *Are we crazy? Why are we doing this? How can I do this without Philip?* Those frantic thoughts were all running through my head. But God was with us, and Kathy's church was praying, so we boarded the MFI flight and headed to Northeast Haiti.

As predicted, Jeanne arrived in Haiti just a few days later. At that time in Haiti, access to information was very limited, so it was difficult to know exactly where Jeanne was or where she was headed. There were no cell phones in Haiti at the time, and the only phones in Terrier Rouge were a couple of satellite phones, which were privately owned, but the public could pay to use them. We tried calling home several times, just to tell everyone we were doing okay and to ask what was happening with the storm, but because of the dense cloud cover, there was no signal. We tried listening to the radio, but all we learned was that 3,000 people had died in the city of Gonaïves when raging flood waters poured out of the mountain on one side of the city heading to the ocean on the other side. Now we were more desperate than ever to communicate with our families at home. We knew if they heard that report, they would be afraid for our lives. But there was still no way to call home.

We tried to do what little work we could, but with the storm around us, schools were closed, the streets were flooded, and no one was venturing out. Kirstin celebrated her birthday during one of Jeanne's downpours, and our sweet Haitian hostess, Marie Noël, celebrated her birthday the next day. Then the weather began to clear, and things calmed down. However, we still had no idea where Jeanne had gone or if she might interfere with our trip back to the U.S. We headed back to the airport in Cap-Haitian a couple of days later and started asking everyone where Jeanne was and what we should expect. We learned Jeanne had turned and was now on her way to West Palm Beach – exactly where we were headed! The pilots were trying to get us back there before Jeanne arrived.

We landed safely in West Palm only to hear the pilots say, "Welcome to West Palm Beach. Now please exit the aircraft because we're evacuating with the planes." We made it back to our hotel and glued ourselves to the television, trying to figure out what was happening. And that's when we saw the power of prayer played out in an incredible way. Now-Hurricane Jeanne had come across the island of Puerto Rico, and the north coast of the Dominican Republic, and then had started across the north coast of Haiti. Then right about at the coordinates of Terrier Rouge, Jeanne made a strange ninety-degree turn and headed straight up into the Caribbean. Then she slowed down and completed a full loop-de-loop on herself before turning again, heading to West Palm. She was expected to make landfall in West Palm the next day, right after our flight was scheduled to depart West Palm heading back to Boston. Kathy's church prayed for us twenty-four hours a day for the duration of our trip. We saw that prayer turn a hurricane. Then slow it down and send it in a circle around itself, to give us the twenty-four hours we needed to get out of West Palm before we would have met up with her again. We laughed when we heard the weather forecaster say, "This is a very unusual track for a storm. We don't often see things like this." But God...

As that story illustrates, prayer is vital in fighting off fear. Praying for ourselves when fear creeps in, as well as asking others to join us in praying through a specific situation where we could give in to fear, is the key to getting through situations where fear could be a factor.

On one of our trips to East Africa, Jamie Dennett, Marilee, and I were checking in for our first flight out of the U.S. When we presented our passports at the check-in desk, the agent looked at my passport and at Marilee's and noticed both of them were damaged. They had a little bit of water damage from previous trips, but all the essential information on the identification page was unaffected. In spite of this, the agent was reluctant to allow us to check in with damaged passports. The airline would be slapped with a $10,000 fine if a passenger arrived at their destination airport and the immigration officials in that country refused to allow the passenger to enter because of a damaged passport.

The agents began to discuss this situation, as did the three of us. After much discussion and a very long wait, a manager was summoned to make the final decision. The manager looked at our passports and decided she would try swiping them through their electronic equipment. If the equipment could read the passports, we would be allowed to check-in for the flight. As soon as I heard this, I started praying silently because my passport had not been successfully swiped for about two years because of the water damage. I had visions of Jamie D and, hopefully, Marilee heading off to East Africa without me because the airline wouldn't let me go with my water-spotted passport.

But when the manager took my passport and swiped it through their equipment, I heard a little "beep." She shook her head and said, "Well, it swiped. So, I guess I can check you in." I smiled, thanked her, and when we had our boarding passes in hand, we quickly headed for the security area before they changed their minds. As we walked away, I told Jamie D and Marilee that God had just performed a miracle because my passport had not swiped properly for the past two years. We all marveled at how God is in control of even the little things like swiping a passport. Later, we found out that long-time volunteer and finance team member, Clemma, had felt compelled to pray for us at that exact time. She had no idea what was going on since we didn't call or message anyone asking for prayer. She simply felt the nudge of the Holy Spirit while we were in that situation and asked God to keep His hand over us as we traveled. And He sure did!

Another example of having others pray for us occurred on one of our trips to Haiti. We were a team of nine, and the time to leave Haiti and return home was approaching. At that time, there was only one road we could take to get from Terrier Rouge back to the airport in Cap-Haitian, and the road went directly through the city of Trou du Nord. While we had been in Haiti, there had been an uprising in Trou du Nord, and the people had completely blocked the road.

No one could get through. We had no idea how we were going to get back to the airport when it was time to go home.

We continued doing what we were in Haiti to do and made it a matter of prayer for the team, but we were trusting God to work it out. As departure day drew closer, we began to get a bit more concerned and decided to contact one person back at home from each of our churches. We sent messages to three people, letting them know what was going on, asking them to pray, but also asking them not to talk to anyone else about it. We didn't want to stir up a spirit of fear among our friends and family back home. We told them it was not yet time to raise the red flag, but if it came to that point, we would contact them again and let them know.

In the meantime, Marie was getting nervous. Pastor Noël was back at their primary home in Cap-Haitian and couldn't get back to Terrier Rouge, so they were trying to figure out what to do. On a previous visit to Haiti, I met a man who was the head of security for the UN forces in the north of Haiti. He told me if we ever needed help, I should contact him. I mentioned this to Marie, so she and a Haitian driver took Matt and me to the UN encampment just outside Terrier Rouge.

When we got there, we asked if the man I had met was there. He wasn't there at the time, but they would tell him I had come by and that we had a problem. When we asked them if there was any way they could help us get back to Cap-Haitian in a day or two, they said they were powerless to do anything. They had all they could do to just keep things in Trou du Nord from escalating, but they thanked us for letting them know we were in Terrier Rouge. Matt and I told them there were nine of us in total, and they said they would keep that in mind as things progressed.

Once we left the camp, Marie had the driver take us to a

tiny road that was just wide enough for one vehicle to pass at a time. As we drove down this lane, which was not much bigger than a donkey track, she told us what Pastor Noël had told her we would have to do when it was time to leave. We would have to go down this track to where the river went through it, then get out of the vehicle and cross through the river on foot since there was no bridge. He would be there to meet us with his vehicle on the other side. Sounded easy enough. The river was shallow with slow-moving water, so we thought we could handle it.

Then we overheard Marie talking to the driver in Creole. I believe she thought we wouldn't understand what they were saying, but we clearly did. They were saying someone would have to go up there ahead of time to make sure there was no trouble. Those who were causing problems in Trou du Nord would not be happy to have our group circumvent their roadblock by finding another way out. Whoever went up there ahead of time to scope things out would have to pay someone off in order to let us pass through without making trouble. Matt and I didn't really like the sound of that.

When we got back to the house and told the team what we would have to do when departure day came, no one was very positive about it. At the time, I had a nasty wound on one of my feet, which Carlyn, Matt's wife, had been doctoring for me. Also, daughter Kirstin was on the team and had just recently announced her pregnancy with our first grandchild. The idea of either of us walking through that nasty water in the river wasn't very encouraging. Matt said he would carry us through it, which led to an evening of silliness as we made up crazy scenarios about how Matt would carry all of us across at the same time, fighting off imaginary snakes in the water. It was silly, but the laughter kept us from becoming too fearful.

Departure day arrived, and it was a Sunday. The road was still blocked, so we contacted the three people at home we had asked to pray and told them *now* it was time to raise the red flag. Since it was a Sunday morning, we asked if they could announce it when they each got to church and ask the whole congregation in each church to pray. At the 10:00 a.m. start of all three church services, everyone in attendance stopped and prayed for God to make a way for us to get out – whether it was going through the river or if God intervened and opened up the road.

We were a bit tense about the situation as we prepared to go to church that morning. Pastor Noël had managed to get to Terrier Rouge by going up to the river on the side he could reach in his car; then left his car there, crossed through the river on foot, and caught a ride to Terrier Rouge on the other side. He was at the mission house in Terrier Rouge with us, preparing to go to church just like everyone else, without any indication that he was concerned about how things would play out when it was time to go. We followed his lead and just kept preparing to go to church.

Suddenly, we heard the sound of large vehicles passing by the front of the house, which sits right on the main road: the same road that was blocked in Trou du Nord just a few miles to the west. We looked out the windows and saw that the vehicles were large UN trucks filled with troops, as well as National police vehicles, and they were all heading toward Trou du Nord. We had no idea what was happening but could only assume things had escalated, which wasn't a comforting thought.

Not long after 9:00 a.m., those same vehicles came back through town in the opposite direction, filled with people who had been arrested in Trou. The vehicles were heading in the direction of Fort Liberty, which is where the prison is located. Then we heard the most incredible news: the road was open! After church, when it was time for us to leave and go back to Cap-Haitian, we drove right through Trou du Nord as if nothing had happened. We could see the evidence of the unrest with vehicles overturned on the side of the road and the remnants of burned tires, but the roadway had been cleared of all that debris, and we drove right through.

A short time later, once we were back in the U.S., my friend Linda, who attends one of the churches that had prayed for us that morning, contacted me. She said she had been thinking about the whole episode and was wondering what time it was when the road finally opened up. I told her we saw the vehicles passing through town the second time – after they had cleared the uprising – a little after 9:00. She seemed deflated when I said that because their service started at 10:00, and that's when they had been praying. She realized everything was already resolved by the time they prayed. I thanked her for praying anyway - and then it hit me. At the time this event happened, the U.S. was on daylight savings time, but Haiti had chosen not to observe it that particular year, which meant they were one hour behind the U.S. When the churches were praying for us at 10:00 that morning, it was only 9:00 in Haiti – exactly the time the uprising had stopped, and the road opened back up. Don't you just love it when God allows us to see His hand in the events around us so clearly?

Probably my favorite example of the power of prayer happened one time when we were visiting Pastor Bamo in Uganda. Our plan was to cross over into the Congo at the Bunagana crossing in North Kivu province to see the children in the program and update their information. We had applied for our visas before making the trip to Africa, and we had received them, but there was conflict in the area of the Bunagana crossing and North Kivu province in general. Rebel forces were in combat with the Congolese forces, and UN troops had been deployed to the area. It seemed as though we would not be able to cross into the Congo after all, even though we had visas.

Pastor Bamo is Congolese and has family in the area we needed to get to, so he kept in communication with them as our scheduled day to cross into Congo approached. They told him things had calmed down a bit, and they thought it would be possible for us to cross over and make it to the village. So, we sat down and had a discussion as a team: three light-skinned American women – Marilee, her friend Donna, and me – and Pastor Bamo. He asked us if we were still willing to cross over into the Congo even with the threat of fighting in the area. All three of us women were in agreement: we were willing to go if he was willing to take us. We knew Bamo would have our safety as his utmost concern. We also knew if God didn't want us to go, there were a thousand ways He could stop us from going. He had already allowed us to obtain visas without which we couldn't even consider crossing. He had allowed Bamo's advisors on the Congo side to tell us it was possible for us to cross. He had subdued the conflict enough for us to even consider crossing. But there was still one obstacle.

Whenever we went into the Congo in the past, Bamo had to borrow a vehicle from someone at the border on the Congolese side and drive us out to the village. With the current situation on the Congo side, he knew there would be no one willing to let him borrow their vehicle and drive through that area to get to the village. We accepted the fact that this obstacle may be the one God would use to keep us from being able to go. But we all prayed and presented our case at His throne. We told Him we were willing to go, and we **would** go unless He closed the door and made it impossible. We knew it could be dangerous, but none of us had fear about it. We simply put the whole situation in God's hands and trusted Him to either work it out for us to go or to shut the door firmly in our faces.

After praying, Bamo suddenly had an idea. In the village we were going to, there is a small field hospital left over from the days when there was a thriving missionary compound there. It's a tiny hospital, but it does have an ambulance. Bamo has many friends in ministry who work at that hospital, so he called one of them and asked if they could send the ambulance to the border to meet us and bring us out there. And they agreed – for a price. But it was a price we were willing and able to pay.

The next morning the four of us headed to the border – after sending messages home letting friends and family know we intended to cross and asking them to pray for us throughout the day. As I mentioned in a previous chapter, when you cross a border by land in Africa, you first have to pass through immigration in the country you are exiting. So our first stop was at immigration in Uganda to get an exit stamp. The immigration officer was incredulous: three light-skinned American women and a Ugandan pastor want to cross over into the Congo?! He asked us if we were sure, and we assured him we knew what we were doing and did, indeed, want to cross. We told him God was with us, and He was the one asking us to go, and we were simply obeying. So he shook his head and stamped the exit stamp in all of our passports.

Then we had to walk through the area of no-man's-land

between Uganda and the Democratic Republic of the Congo. It would not be an exaggeration to say all eyes were on our unusual group as we walked across the border into the Congo and entered the immigration building on the Congolese side.

As you would expect, the immigration officials were not sure they wanted to allow our conspicuous group to enter the Congo. So, the main official took Pastor Bamo and went into a private office, leaving Marilee, Donna, and me sitting in the main area with several guards. Our internal dialogue during that awkward time was to keep silent, be pleasant, and be compliant but assured that we would be allowed into the country.

After what seemed like a very long time, Pastor Bamo and the official came out of the office, and we were allowed to enter the Congo. The ambulance arrived, and the four of us got into the back, but it was a different type of vehicle than the ambulances we have in the U.S. This one was more like a large SUV with windows all around. We sat on two padded benches in the back and took in the visual display outside the vehicle. Hundreds of UN troops, hundreds of Congolese troops, and masses of internally displaced people filled the small road on which we had to drive. It seemed impossible to think we would be able to drive through that mass of humanity, but the crowds simply parted when they saw the ambulance, and we drove right through. There were also some road blocks on that road with a long pole which stretched across the road. But whenever the people manning the road blocks saw the ambulance approaching, they simply raised the pole and let us pass without stopping. The whole thing brought to mind the story of Moses parting the Red Sea and the Israelites crossing unharmed. Donna, Marilee, and I couldn't keep from laughing with joy when we thought about the miracle God was providing.

We arrived in the village without ever having to stop for anyone, got our equipment out of the ambulance, and started to set everything up. While we were setting up, I heard what I thought was the rumble of thunder in the distance, and I looked up at Bamo. We knew from past experience if it rains when we are in the village, we have to pack everything up and leave as quickly as possible. The grassy track that passes for a road becomes impassible in the rain very quickly. I was honestly disappointed God would allow us to get all the way out there only to be forced to pack it in and leave because of rain. When I looked at Bamo with that unspoken thought obviously showing on my face, he simply smiled at me and said, "They asked me not to tell you that you would hear that out here. It's not thunder. The rebel forces are fighting the Congolese troops in that area across the valley. That sound is heavy artillery."

We never saw any evidence of the fighting, but the rumble of artillery continued the entire time we were out there. We never had to stop, we never felt fearful, and we completed the task we had to do that day, which is nothing short of miraculous. When it was time to leave, we loaded ourselves and our equipment back into the ambulance and made it safely back to the border without incident.

The guards at the Congolese immigration office were obviously surprised to see us back at the border even though we told them our plan was to go out to the village and come back the same day. We know they did not expect us to get back safely, and their surprise was apparent on their faces. However, nothing tops the reaction of the immigration official back on the Uganda side of the border. His face registered more shock than surprise, and he exclaimed in a loud voice, *"You're back!!!!!"* We calmly told him we knew we'd be back because it was God who was sending us. And we could confidently say that, without fear, only because of the prayers of those who prayed for us faithfully throughout the entire day.

People have often asked me if I was afraid that day or have said I must be brave to do something like that, but my answer is always the same. "God has already planned out the exact day, time, and place of my death, and it is immaterial to me how it happens. I could die in my sleep in my bed at home at age ninety-nine, or I could die as a result of a roadside bomb in the Congo. Neither one makes any difference to me. Because I know the end result will be the same no matter how it happens, and that's the only thing that matters."

But I do have to share one special moment that happened on this remarkable day because it was a powerful demonstration of how God revealed Himself to us, letting us know – without a doubt – that He was right there with us.

Just before we got to the village in the Congo to set up for the day, Bamo asked the ambulance driver to stop at a small shack where beverages were sold. He wanted to get us something to drink while we were working with the children. So, he exited the ambulance through the back door which was at the back end of the vehicle. When he got out, he left the door open and there were a few children in the area between the back of the ambulance and the front of the shack. A small boy who looked to be no more than three or four years old noticed the three light-skinned women sitting in the back of the ambulance and did something incredibly powerful. He approached the back of the ambulance with a look of concern on his face. But instead of asking us for something, which is a common experience, he held out a small piece of his bread, offering it to us. I have never forgotten the look of concern and compassion on the face of that small boy, and I believe it was God's way of demonstrating to us He had His hand over us that day.

"Yea, though I walk through the valley of the shadow of death, I will fear no evil; For You are with me; Your rod and Your staff, they comfort me." (Psalm 23:4 NKJV)

The little Congolese boy offering us a piece of his bread

17

WHEN THINGS GO WRONG

"What would you do if something bad happened while you were in a Third World country? Aren't you afraid something will go wrong?"

Yes, sometimes bad things happen. They can occur in the U.S. too. We don't need to travel to another country to have bad things happen or to have plans go wrong. Those are the results of living in a fallen world. Being in another country can sometimes make it more difficult to deal with those things when they happen, but it is not something we're afraid of, and it is certainly not a reason for us to ignore God's leading.

When Philip and I made our first trip to Haiti, we certainly considered the potential for danger. We were going to a place neither of us had been before and we had heard some bad things about it. We went to a bookstore[1] to find a travel guide we could read to learn more. We couldn't find one on Haiti, so we picked up one on the Caribbean and started to thumb through. As we came across the different sections for each Caribbean country, we would read a little about their history, some places of interest, local foods, and customs, etc. We were eagerly anticipating finding the Haiti section in the book to see what it said. When we finally located it, all it said was: "Haiti – Don't." I am not kidding. The heading at the top of the page said "Haiti" and the only word on the entire page was "Don't." We put the book back on the shelf and began to have some fear about making the trip even though we knew it was something God wanted us to do. We counted the cost and decided to go anyway, had our wills drawn up (seriously!), and left for Haiti simply trusting God to bring us back home again.

Philip and I had a bad experience on a trip that happened right here in the U.S. We were on our way home from visiting our partners in Indonesia and had an overnight layover in Los Angeles. When making the reservations for the trip, we considered getting a hotel room for our layover in LA but, in the interest of being frugal, decided against it. However, once we arrived at the airport in LA, we were exhausted both physically and mentally, and it was late at night. We decided to get a hotel room.

I went to the information desk in the airport and asked for information on area hotels. The agent indicated a row of phones over by a window, each one a direct line to a hotel near the airport. We went over to the phones and started calling each one, but there were no available rooms – until we got to the last phone. That hotel had a room and had a shuttle, which came to the airport on a regular schedule. When their shuttle arrived, we got on and were thankful to be heading to a hotel where we could get some rest.

Our hopes were dashed when we arrived at the hotel. It was in a very run-down area, which felt completely unsafe. Guests weren't even allowed to enter the lobby. Our check-in process happened outside through a protective plexiglass shield with a pass-through at the bottom. When we arrived at our room, we were shocked to discover *six* different doors that led into the room; some from the hallway, some from a green area outside, and some from adjoining rooms. We put chairs up against as many as we could.

We hadn't had anything to eat and noticed a Taco Bell next to the hotel, so we walked over there to grab a bite to eat before turning in. The inside dining area was closed, but the drive-thru window was still open, so we went and stood in the drive-thru line, expecting to be kicked out of line for not being in a vehicle. No one seemed to care.

As we stood there taking in our surroundings, we noticed the Taco Bell sign was on a very tall pole with other signs on it. Another sign saying "Adult Books" was directly underneath the Taco Bell sign, giving the impression this Taco Bell was also an adult bookstore. Across the busy street from the Taco Bell was a liquor store. While we were standing in line, a man who appeared to be very inebriated exited the liquor store. At that very moment, a young man whizzed by on his bike, grabbing the intoxicated man's belongings. The man started screaming and yelling that he'd been robbed, but no one responded. We half expected to witness a drive-by shooting while standing there: the neighborhood was that sketchy.

We survived the rest of our evening and tried to check out in the early hours of the morning to return to the airport for our flight. However, the front desk was unmanned, and there was no shuttle in sight. While we stood there trying to figure out how to resolve this unexpected crisis, we saw a taxi drive by and stop at a gas station on the other side of the street, just past the hotel. Philip left me standing in the hotel parking lot with our hand baggage while he ran across the street and down the sidewalk to catch that taxi and ask for a ride back to the airport. He was successful, and we were extremely thankful for not only having a ride back to the airport, but also surviving our stay in a dangerous part of LA.

We also have other examples of bad things happening over the years. For instance, Wanda's suitcase did not arrive back at her home airport with her. Instead, it took a two-week world tour, which included a visit to Lima, Peru, before returning to her at her home in Peru, Maine. Another time Marilee's suitcase never made it to the airport in Manila with her. It arrived there a few days later, but the airline wouldn't deliver it to her because the mission house she stayed at was five hours from the airport. Marilee spent the entire trip borrowing clothes from her much-taller teammate, Sherlyn. She also went shopping with some of our Filipino friends, but finding clothing in Filipino stores that fit an American body wasn't very easy. She managed though – and that's the real point – and met up with her suitcase again when they went back to the Manila airport to go home.

We have also been robbed a few times. While walking through an open-air market in Guatemala, team member Kara knew she needed to be careful with her backpack, so she was wearing it in front of her instead of on her back. That worked well, until someone stopped short in front of her, causing her to bump into them. When the person walked away, Kara discovered the bottom of her backpack had been slashed open, and several valuable items were gone.

Another time, also in a crowded market in Guatemala, Jamie Dennett was walking through a narrow passageway trying to exit a building. The passageway had vendors on both sides, and people were walking in both directions through this passageway, coming in and out of the market. Jamie was careful to keep her cross-body purse in front of her as she walked through. However, once she got outside, she looked down and noticed that her purse was on her side now, instead of in front of her, and the zipper was open. Her wallet was gone.

On one of our Haiti trips, we were riding in the back of an open pickup truck – the type that is frequently used for public transportation (called a "tap-tap"). This one was not a public tap-tap but was driven by a friend of ours. As the vehicle passed through a small town it slowed down to go over a speed bump. When it slowed, a young man jumped on the back bumper of the truck. He had a goofy grin on his face, so I assumed he thought the tap-tap was a public one, and he wanted to get on with all the blancs. I spoke to him in Creole, telling him it was not a public vehicle and he needed to get down, but he just stood there smiling that silly smile. Since the vehicle was still moving slowly, I wanted to give him a little shove to make him get off the bumper. I resisted the urge because I thought it wouldn't be a very nice thing to do. Instead, I turned away from him so I could lean over the side of the truck and bang on it, signaling the driver that we needed to stop. As soon as I turned my back to the young man, he leaned into the truck and grabbed Lorna's backpack. She held onto the handle for dear life, but he was younger and stronger, pulling her off the bench we were sitting on and landing her on the floor of the truck bed. Then he twisted the bag, which broke her fingers and forced her to let go. Once he had the bag, he jumped down off the bumper, ran back, and jumped on a motorcycle that was following us, and they took off. Thankfully, she had nothing of value in her bag, but it was still painful for Lorna and upset all of us.

Another team was robbed while they were sleeping. A man broke into the house where they were staying and quietly tiptoed through their bedrooms, helping himself to their valuables and cash while they slept. They were thankful no one woke up until after he had exited the house and also thankful he didn't harm anyone.

We have also learned the hard way what to do when you are tear-gassed. Several times when we've been in Haiti, there has been rioting in the street where the mission house is located. The street is the main road through the city and the main road that leads to the Dominican border. When tensions mount, they tend to boil over right in front of the mission house. On a few occasions, tear gas has been used on the rioting crowds, and the gas has inadvertently drifted into the house. Our Haitian friends always have cut limes ready to rub on our eyes because the citrus cuts through the burning of the tear gas.

Yes, sometimes bad things happen when we're on a trip, but these kinds of things can, and do, happen anywhere – even here in the U.S.

Sometimes we have problems created by team members – more often with adult team members than with children or teens. My theory is that children and teens are generally more accustomed to listening to instruction from someone in authority, like a team leader, while adults want to make their own decisions or do things their own way.

Philip was leading a team once and had an adult team member look him in the face and say, "You're not the boss of me." We have had other team members who came with their own agenda and tried starting new projects in the name of the ministry without consulting us, projects we would never have approved. These kinds of issues caused us to grow up as a ministry, setting new policies and developing a trip application with more in-depth screening questions. In at least one instance, we feel confident the application saved us from dealing with another difficult team member.

When this person filled out their application, they gave some very telling answers. They first indicated their strength was their natural leadership ability and that people naturally followed them. Then they indicated their weakness was that they had difficulty letting other people be in charge. This person was only twenty-one years old. The straw that broke the camel's back was when another one of their answers made it clear they had their own agenda they hoped to accomplish on the trip - an agenda that had nothing to do with our purpose in going. That application saved us from dealing with a whole host of potential problems when the person was denied a spot on the team.

Sometimes problems are unwittingly created by team members. On one Haiti trip, our team brought a large number of soccer balls to leave with Pastor Noël to take to the school. Throughout our time there, a couple of the young men on the team would take a ball and go out in the street and play soccer with some of the older boys and young men in the community. On our last night in Haiti, they played soccer again. At the end of the game, the young men from our team let one of the young Haitian men - a friend of ours - keep the ball. It seemed harmless, and if I had been with them, I probably would have told them it was fine to do that.

When the young men from our team returned to the mission house, a large number of the Haitian young men came back with them. They were all standing on the front porch of the mission house, visiting with one another along with some of the girls on our team. Inside the house, the rest of us were re-inflating the remainder of the soccer balls (which we transported to Haiti deflated) so we could leave them with Pastor Noël ready to be used. The Haitian young men on the porch saw us inflating all those soccer balls and assumed we would be giving them out. We told them they were for the school, but things on the porch started to get a bit out of hand. I asked our team members to come inside and close the door hoping that would put an end to it. It didn't.

The Haitian young men simply walked around to the back of the house and let themselves into the back courtyard. There were a lot more of them by now, and they made Marie very nervous because she didn't know most of them. She asked one of the young men who helped around the house (I'll call him Mark) to make them leave. Mark directed them all back out of the gate, but once they got outside, things heated up again. Nasty things were said, a few punches were exchanged, and then the young men began to disperse.

Then Mark went up onto the roof of the house and dropped a cement block off the roof when the young men passed by. It didn't hit anyone, and I don't believe Mark intended to hit anyone, but to discourage them from coming back. However, there were policemen sitting on the porch of the house next door to the mission house, and they saw what happened. They arrested Mark, and he was beaten and thrown in jail. All this started when someone gave away a soccer ball…

Sometimes our plans go wrong. One time we were in Haiti during Tropical Storm Noel. The storm wasn't too bad in Haiti, but it passed through the Bahamas, dumping a significant amount of rain as it moved north of Haiti. We were flying with MFI that year and they had to stop in the Bahamas to refuel the plane. With all the rain from the storm, the runway in the Bahamas was underwater, making MFI's flight impossible. They managed to contact us to tell us they would not be able to come to Haiti to bring us home on our scheduled departure day. This might not sound like much of a problem, but most of our team was from the northeast U.S. MFI only flies us from Fort Pierce, Florida to Haiti and then back again. The team members have to take separate flights from the Northeast down to Florida. With our MFI flight being rescheduled, all the team's commercial flights within the U.S. had to be rescheduled as well: a very difficult thing to do from Haiti at that time due to spotty phone service. Fortunately, we were able to contact Henry Cooper back in Maine, and he took care of everything for us.

Our plans went wrong when we had a trip to Haiti planned for March 15, 2004. On February twenty-ninth of that same year, Haiti experienced a political coup. The president left the country, and anyone who was considered part of the government fled, including the police. Haiti has no military, so this left no one "minding the store," so to speak. The UN made plans to mobilize and send troops in to keep the peace. Before that could be organized, four countries volunteered to send in troops - the U.S., Canada, France, and Chile - with France taking responsibility for the Northeast Department, where Terrier Rouge is located.

With all this going on, Pastor Noël managed to get a message to us telling us not to come, so we put our plans on hold. However, just six weeks after the coup, after receiving another message from Pastor Noël asking us to come, we made the trip with a revised team. Because several of the original team members were not able to change their work schedules, the team had decreased in size, but there were still enough of us to do what we needed to do.

That team experienced a lot of difficult things due to the instability in Haiti. Some of the difficulties we experienced were due to the lack of law and order, along with acts of vigilante justice, but some of the difficulties were of a spiritual nature. One of our children was on that team and struggled with some of the things she experienced. In hindsight, it might not have been the wisest decision to go so soon after a political overthrow, but we believed it was what God wanted us to do.

On another Haiti trip, we had team members coming from several different parts of the U.S. and Canada. This meant I had to book separate reservations for each group based on which departure airport they would use. As we were leaving Haiti, each group checked in for their return flights at the same time. When the group returning to Maine was checked in, some of them were given boarding passes for their onward flights, and some were given seat request cards. (A seat request card indicates they had a reserved seat on the flight but had not yet been given an actual seat assignment.) However, the youngest member of our team, Mace, who was seventeen years old at the time and traveling without a parent, was not given either a boarding pass or a seat request card for any of his onward flights. Without either of those documents, he would not be able to pass through security before those flights.

I was very concerned about this situation because I would not be with their group once they got back to the U.S. and had to make those flights. I was living in Florida by that time and would not be going back to Maine with their group. I approached the Haitian man working at the ticket counter and asked him why he had not given Mace the documents he needed. He was quite dismissive and said, without any explanation, he could not give him the documents. Not one to be easily dismissed in these types of situations, I told the man Mace was a minor traveling without a parent, and he could not be left on his own without either a boarding pass or a seat request card. The man would not be moved. In fact, he began to ignore me and continued shuffling papers without any apparent purpose. I continued to insist he give Mace the documents he needed, but he continued to ignore me. At that point, I simply said, "Well, you can ignore me if you like, but we're not moving from this spot until you take care of this matter."

He didn't care. He went right on shuffling papers and didn't care that he wouldn't be able to wait on anyone else until we moved, which we were not going to do. It became a stand-off with him ignoring us while we stood there, determined not to move until he took care of the situation.

After what seemed like twenty minutes had passed, the man got on the phone. I could hear and understand his conversation, and it had nothing to do with our situation. While he was talking, he stopped for a moment and asked me for Mace's passport, which I handed to him. A minute or two later, he pushed some buttons, and a document popped out of the machine behind the counter. Still on the phone, he handed me the document and Mace's passport without comment. I looked at the document, expecting to see a seat request card, but it wasn't. It was an actual boarding pass! I couldn't help myself. The pent up frustration over the whole situation got the best of me, and I cried out, "Well, lookie there! You *can* do it!!" while team member Laura gently ushered me away from the desk.

While on one of our trips to India with our previous India coordinator, JD Last, she received a text from her husband in the middle of the night. His text simply said, "There's been an accident. Can you call me?" JD woke me up and asked if she could use the ministry's phone. I gave her the phone, and she quickly called home only to discover that her mother had been in a boating accident and had passed away. It was horrible. We often think about things like this when we're on our trips but couldn't imagine actually having to face it.

JD and her family had to make a difficult decision: should JD try to leave India and come home now, or should she stick it out and fly home on the day we already booked? Leaving early wouldn't be easy. Where we stay is many hours from the airport. If she tried to go home early she would most likely have to pay more and might have to fly stand-by. Flying stand-by meant she might not get home any earlier than originally planned and she would be exhausted. In light of this, the decision was made for her to stay and fly home as planned. Every evening they would communicate by phone and online, making the necessary final arrangements, but it was really a tough situation.

After several days, it was time for us to leave. We boarded our first flight, which would take us to another city in India before heading on to Paris and then Boston. When we got to our first layover in India and went to check-in for our Paris flight, we discovered the flight had been canceled. There were airline strikes in Paris, so no flights were going there. The only flights they could offer us would get JD back home after the scheduled time of her mother's memorial service. No way would we accept those offers! Again, having learned how to be polite but persistent in these types of situations, I told the ticket agent she would have to come up with something better so JD would not miss her mother's memorial service.

Understanding the gravity of our situation, the ticket agent did her best but could not find anything else on their airline (which I will not name). She told us she would do something they don't normally allow. She booked us on another airline, which was not one of their partner airlines. The other airline had an available flight with connections to get us to Boston in time, but we would have to go to their counter and check-in with them. She gave us the itinerary, along with directions to the other airline counter, and off we went. It was on the opposite side of the terminal: a long walk with all our hand baggage.

When we tried to check-in at the other airline's check-in desk, the agent asked us if we had bags to check-in. We told her we had already checked them in when we boarded our first flight. They were supposed to be checked through to our final destination. However, she told us we could not check-in without those bags, which we had no way to get. She told me I would have to go back to our original airline (which I'll call Airline A) and ask them to transfer the bags to the new airline (which I'll call Airline B). She also said that our seats were not guaranteed until we could check-in.

I knew we *had* to have those seats. I left JD at Airline B to hold our place in line while I ran back over to Airline A as fast as I could, carrying a twenty-pound equipment backpack. Airline A said it wasn't their problem, and Airline B would have to take care of it. I went back to Airline B, where I got the same response: the other airline would have to take care of it. I was sent back and forth, from one side of the terminal to the other - running every time and carrying that heavy backpack - too many times to count.

I was getting frustrated and upset that we might lose the seats causing JD to miss her mother's memorial service. When Airline B told me to go back to Airline A yet again, I passed a manager for Airline B on my way there. I stopped and told him about our situation, with desperation in my voice, but he had no mercy. Instead, he began to yell at me, telling me it wasn't Airline B's problem. He told me I had to go back to Airline A and get a manager, bring them back with me to Airline B, and then *maybe* he would help me. By this time, I had reached my breaking point. I looked at him with daggers in my eyes, shook my finger at him, and shouted, "I'm going to go back over to Airline A! I'm *going* to find a manager to come back here with me! And then you're *going* to do something to help us, *or it's not going to be pretty*!!!" Philip has asked me what I meant by that or what I intended to do. I have no idea. It was simply the worst thing I could think of to say at that moment.

I went back to Airline A, desperately asking for a manager to come back to Airline B with me. They finally found someone, and when we got there, the two managers began to argue with one another, with Airline B winning the fight. JD and I didn't care, though. We were just happy to finally be allowed to check-in and get those desperately-needed seats.

On one of our Haiti trips, I woke up early one morning - before most of the team members were awake - and listened to the voicemail messages on the ministry phone. I sat there listening to a message from a woman who identified herself as Karen's niece while looking across the room at Karen's face as she woke up. The niece's message asked us to let Karen know that her mother had passed away unexpectedly. I was devastated, knowing I had some information I needed to share with Karen that would be terrible for her to hear while looking at her sitting on her bed smiling at me. I couldn't do it. I decided to wake up her husband and let him listen to the message so he could tell her what had happened. It was so hard for both of them. They decided they needed to go home as soon as possible. I was able to contact MFI to arrange for them to fly out the next day. They were able to contact the commercial airline they were booked on to return to California from Florida once MFI got them there. It really wasn't that difficult to get it all arranged, but we were all sad, not only about what had happened, but also because they would have to leave us.

Early the next morning, before the sun was up, a group of ladies from the church was walking around the community - zone by zone - singing hymns and praying in each one. This is something they do once each week, and the day Karen and Steve had to leave us was one of the group's scheduled days. By the time they reached our zone, the sun had come up, but it was still very early. They stood in the road outside the house singing beautiful hymns in Creole and then praying. Then they asked if they could come inside and pray for Karen. Marie welcomed them in, and we all went into the dining room to greet them. Karen sat in one of the dining room chairs while the women all sang again, then laid hands on her and prayed for her. It was incredibly moving and a powerful demonstration of the love we share for one another because of our common bond in Jesus Christ.

Yes, sometimes our plans go wrong. It's never easy when that happens, and sometimes I don't react very well. Sometimes we find ourselves in situations that make us uncomfortable. To quote Francis Chan, "But God doesn't call us to be comfortable. He calls us to trust Him so completely that we are unafraid to put ourselves in situations where we will be in trouble if He doesn't come through."[2] We know every situation we confront is one that has already passed through God's hands. Yes, some of those situations may make us uncomfortable. Some of them may be difficult for us to handle. Some of them may challenge us to respond appropriately. But, we know God is with us in each one and has His purposes in them. It is up to us to live up to the challenge and grow as we continue to walk in the good works He has planned for us, whether they go according to our plan or not.

"God is our refuge and strength, an ever-present help in trouble. Therefore we will not fear, though the earth give way and the mountains fall into the heart of the sea, though its waters roar and foam and the mountains quake with their surging." (Psalm 46:1-3 NIV)

JD praying with one of the elderly ladies in India

18

COLOSSAL DO-OVER

"Have you ever missed an opportunity to do something to help someone and then regretted it?"

Oh boy, have I. If we're honest with ourselves, we could all say yes to this question.

It was in 2004, and I was flying with Missionary Flights International back to the U.S. with our small team of ladies. On the flight was an older Haitian couple. We didn't really talk with them much because we were all focused on getting back before Hurricane Jeanne caught up with us.

When we arrived at the terminal in West Palm Beach, our team ended up in the same shuttle van as this elderly couple who were going to the same hotel where we were staying. I found myself at the check-in desk checking in our team, while the elderly Haitian couple was also checking in at the desk at the same time. There were two desk clerks that evening, so we were both waited on at the same time, the couple standing at the left side of the desk, and me standing on the right.

While checking in, I couldn't help but overhear the elderly couple had been invited to the U.S. by someone to speak somewhere. This other person was supposed to have paid for their hotel room, but they had neglected to do so. The couple was upset and didn't know what to do and just kept telling the desk clerk that their room was supposed to be paid for already. Deep down in my spirit, I kept feeling a nudge telling me to pay for their room. I was trying to ignore it, telling myself I would be embarrassed if they knew I was listening to their conversation or that someone else would take care of it. I shut out their conversation and simply focused on the clerk handling our check-in process and ignored that very strong prompting to step in and help the couple.

Once we were checked in and headed to our room, grief and guilt overwhelmed me. I had to stop and confess to the team that I had just royally blown it. They were all kind and compassionate and told me not to be too hard on myself, but I knew, without a doubt, I had just told the Holy Spirit to leave me alone, and I regretted it big time.

Fast forward to one year later, in December of 2005, when I was, once again, flying back to the U.S. on Missionary Flights International – this time with Holly and Bea. While we were waiting to board the flight in Cap-Haitian, I noticed a young woman, probably about the same age as Holly, who was sitting near us in the waiting area. She was sitting with an older woman who turned out to be her aunt. The young woman had just spent a month in Haiti, visiting her aunt, and was returning to the U.S. alone on the same flight we were taking.

When it was time to board, the aunt handed over her niece to another older woman on our flight, a friend of the aunt. This older woman would make sure the young woman navigated her way back to West Palm Beach, but after that, she would be on her own.

On our journey back to the U.S., we discovered the young woman had several other flights to make after she arrived in West Palm Beach before she would actually arrive at her home airport. We also learned she was staying overnight in West Palm in the same hotel where we were staying. She told us her name was Heather, and we quickly invited her to join us in our room for some pizza once we got to the hotel and checked in. She said she would love to, but she didn't have any money – not even a single penny in her pocket – since she had just spent a month in Haiti and had gone through all the money she brought with her. We told her it didn't matter; there would be plenty of pizza to share, and she was still welcome to join us.

We arrived in West Palm, took that same shuttle to the hotel together, and then found ourselves at the check-in desk at the same time: Heather standing at the left side of the desk, and me on the right. In the course of both of us checking in at the same time, I couldn't help but overhear that Heather's room was supposed to be paid for, but it was not. I knew she had no money, so she would have no way to pay for it. Then I felt that nudge again, that nudge telling me to step in and pay for her room.

Before I could take even half a second to consider the nudge, my head snapped up, and I heard these words loudly coming out of my mouth, as I had to hold myself back from jumping over the desk – *"Wait!!! I will pay for her room!!!"* Heather looked up at me, a bit startled, and said no, that wouldn't be necessary. She would figure it out. I just laughed and said, "Oh no, honey. You have *no* idea what's going on here, but I *am paying for your room*!!"

God doesn't often give us a "do-over" like this, and I was not going to mess it up this time. I had not forgotten what I had done just a year before. Even though I had confessed it and repented, there was still a feeling of regret over it. Now that I had a chance to do it right, I was going to do it no matter what.

After checking in, Heather came to our room, and we all shared some pizza before she went to her own room, and we all went to bed. The following morning, we all had breakfast together in the hotel and then took the same shuttle back to the airport. We said our good-byes to Heather at the entrance, and then our group checked in for our flight and got into the line for security.

Once we were in line, a thought popped into my head. *Why didn't we give her some money??* She still had several flights to take before she made it home. It was going to be an all-day thing for her, but she had no money for food or anything. I had just shared this thought with Holly and Bea, and we were kicking ourselves for not thinking of it sooner when, standing right there – right next to where we were standing in a serpentine security line – was Heather! I couldn't believe it! God had given me *another* chance to do it right!

We forced some money into her hands before the line moved, and we lost sight of her again. We went through security and walked to our gate, feeling much better about the whole situation. Then Bea looked down at the box of leftover pizza she had brought with us from the hotel and said, *"Why didn't we give her the pizza??"*

Just then, we heard an announcement at another gate near ours. They were calling Heather's flight. Just as we figured out which gate the announcement came from, there was Heather – standing right there waiting to board. Bea ran over to her, shoved the pizza box in her hand, hugged her, and ran back to our gate. The last time we ever saw her, she was boarding a flight with a big smile on her face carrying a box of leftover pizza.

I have often wondered what became of her. We exchanged contact info, but we never heard from her again. Maybe she was an angel. Who knows? I just know I am very thankful for the second chance God gave me with Heather. And, if you're Heather and you're reading this, I would love to hear from you!

We all miss opportunities to do good to those around us. Either we miss seeing those opportunities, or we're too busy. Sometimes we're just embarrassed, like I was, to step up and act. Sometimes we simply don't want to. There are too many reasons to list, but I think we can all remember a time when we missed an opportunity to bless someone. The point is this; God doesn't always give us such an obvious chance to try again as the one He gave me with Heather – a colossal do-over. When He does give you an opportunity like that, don't miss it a second time. Just do it.

"Do not forget to show hospitality to strangers, for by so doing some people have shown hospitality to angels without knowing it." (Hebrews 13:2 NIV)

"Therefore, as we have opportunity, let us do good to all people, especially to those who belong to the family of believers." (Galatians 6:10 NIV)

Heather (in back) with the woman who was helping her navigate her way back to the U.S. I have no idea why I took this photo. We had not spoken to Heather at all before I took it. For some inexplicable reason, I felt compelled to turn around and sneak this photo of them while we were walking out to board the MFI flight in Cap-Haitian. At the time I took this, I had no idea what God had planned. But God...

19

NOT SO AMAZING

"You are such an amazing person!"

I cringe when people say that to me because no, I'm not. But, I serve a God who is beyond amazing. Anything that could be labeled "amazing" that happens when I am serving Him is only because He is the One who brought about an amazing outcome. It has very little to do with me.

I love to learn different languages. I wouldn't call myself fluent in anything other than English yet, but I can hold my own in Haitian Creole. I understand about seventy-five percent of what is said to me in Spanish, even though I still struggle to come up with my own words in response. I could carry on a simple conversation in French as long as we were talking in the present tense. I'm also dabbling in Italian and Portuguese too. This is another area where I've learned just enough to be dangerous.

Early on in our ministry in Haiti, I was trying very hard to learn to speak Creole. Interviewing the children did a lot to help me accomplish that goal, but I was a long way from being able to have an actual conversation. One day during

those early years, we stopped at a gas station in Haiti. I
needed to use the restroom, so I decided to try out my very-
basic Creole skills. I got out of the vehicle and approached a
Haitian woman who was an attendant at the gas station. I
asked her where the bathroom was located – in Creole. I
was astounded when she smiled and answered me, also in
Creole, telling me where I would find the bathroom. I was
even more astounded when I understood her answer!

I asked Philip to go with me to the area she indicated
because I didn't think it was a good idea to walk over there
alone. While we made our way to the bathroom, I was
patting myself on the back, congratulating myself for having
my first Creole conversation with a complete stranger and
without anyone to help me with a translation. I was so
pleased with myself I was practically floating as we
approached the bathroom – just reveling in my success with
Creole – and thinking way too much of myself while
doing it.

The door to the bathroom was a very heavy, very large,
solid iron door without any opening in it. As I was inside
the bathroom, closing the door, I realized it was going to be
very difficult to see in there because there was no light other
than a tiny sliver of daylight streaming in under the door. I
scoped out the surroundings to make sure I knew where
everything was before I closed that hefty door and slid the
massive iron bolt across to lock it. I managed to do what I
went in there to do, without incident, and made my way
back to the door. Then I realized something horrifying – I
absolutely could *not* get that bolt to slide back so I could
open the door and get out of the bathroom.

I pulled and pulled and shoved and tried to jiggle the
bolt and did everything I could think of, but it wouldn't
budge at all. Panic started to rise in me as I imagined myself

being trapped in that dark, smelly bathroom forever. I called out to Philip to help me, but being the practical guy that he is, he simply informed me there was nothing he could do from the outside, and I was just going to have to keep trying. *"But it won't move!!! I can't get out of this bathroom!!!"* I had visions of workmen being summoned with blowtorches to cut the metal door open to set me free, and the panic continued to build. *Of course it would come to this!! Me, the one who finds potty humor way too funny, gets trapped forever in a gas station restroom in Haiti!!* That was the overwhelming thought in my head as the panic took complete control while I continued trying to move that bolt. Perhaps it was the adrenalin created by the panic, or perhaps God decided I had learned my lesson because suddenly that bolt let go and slid across the door, and I was free. Fresh air and sunshine were never more welcome than when that bathroom finally let me go. The pride I had previously taken in myself was replaced by complete embarrassment from panicking over being trapped in a restroom. I was taken down a notch or two, and that's a good thing.

A very similar incident took place when Philip and I had that first, very emotional, entry into the country of Rwanda. We were flying high from the emotion of a long-held dream being realized as we took our first steps in Rwanda. We were looking around and comparing everything we saw to what we had learned doing our research before making the trip. We made our way to the immigration building and officially entered the country, then had to stand and wait on the lawn of the building for a van that would take us to Kigali. Our imaginations were spinning with the thought of finally making it to Kigali when I realized I should probably try to find a bathroom to use before getting in a van for a ride that would be a few hours long. I asked Bamo if there was a bathroom there at immigration. He said there was, but it was necessary to get a key from one of the immigration officers first because it would be locked. He asked if I wanted help with that since the conversation would have to take place in French, but still feeling elated by actually being in Rwanda, I told him I could handle it myself.

I went up to the immigration window and, in French, asked for the key to the restroom. Again, pride swelled in me when the officer not only understood my question and gave me the key, but I also understood his response when he told me how to find the facilities. I walked off thinking way too much of myself – again – and made my way to the "bathroom". Imagine my surprise when I discovered it was simply a row of wooden latrines set up on a little ridge behind the immigration building as though they were on display. I chose one that appeared to be empty, put the key in the lock, and opened it. That's when I discovered there was no actual toilet or squatty potty, or even a raised platform with a hole in it like the latrines I had used in the U.S. No, this one simply had a hole cut in the middle of the wooden floor.

I was still carrying the key, which was attached to a large piece of wood so it couldn't be easily stolen or put in a pocket and forgotten. Plus, I was wearing a sweater tied around my waist and a cross-body bag with all my personal items in it. Trying to get myself into the proper position over that hole without dropping anything or having any of those items fall off me and into the hole was complicated, to say the least. Again, it was another bathroom with no light, so when the door was closed, it was completely dark in there. I had to figure out how to maneuver myself into position while the door was still slightly open, so I could see what I was doing and not fall into the hole. Once I got everything successfully situated, I went to close the door and lock it. It was then I discovered the door did not latch on the inside. The only way to completely latch it was to lock it with the key from the outside. It struck me as odd that the main concern seemed to be securing the facilities from the outside to keep people out, but once they were inside, there was no thought of securing them in there while they did their business.

There I was, trying to decide what to do in this strange situation. I ended up bending forward at the waist, holding the door closed by pressing the top of my head against the door. It was while I was doing my business in this ungainly position, trying to keep myself from falling in the hole in the dark, trying to keep from dropping anything into the hole that wasn't supposed to go in there, and trying to keep the door shut with my head, that I realized: "Well, I wanted to come to Rwanda, and here I am!" All I could do was laugh. I had taken way too much pride in our accomplishments: getting ourselves to Rwanda at last, having a conversation in French with a stranger, and finding the bathroom on my own. But God gave me an experience in the latrine, which took me down a notch or two, and that's a good thing.

The point of these two stories is to illustrate that I am nothing special in and of myself. I am a grown woman who finds potty humor to be way too funny, who can easily get too full of myself, who often has difficulty thinking before I speak, and can be impulsive and impatient. The list of my flaws could go on and on, but the point is this – God chooses the most unlikely people to accomplish *His* purposes. I would be very near the top of a list of unlikely choices, but when He chooses to use cracked clay pots like me, it becomes very evident to anyone who is watching that it's *only* because of Him that we can do any of the things we do. We are not so special or so amazing – *But God Is.* The amazing thing is that He chooses to use us and allows us to be a small part of what He is accomplishing around the world.

"Brothers and sisters, think of what you were when you were called. Not many of you were wise by human standards; not many were influential; not many were of noble birth. But God chose the foolish things of the world to shame the wise; God chose the weak things of the world to shame the strong. God chose the lowly things of this world and the despised things—and the things that are not—to nullify the things that are, so that no one may boast before him. It is because of him that you are in Christ Jesus, who has become for us wisdom from God—that is, our righteousness, holiness and redemption. Therefore, as it is written: 'Let the one who boasts boast in the Lord.'" (1 Corinthians 1:26-31 NIV)

Hamming it up for the camera after a hair-raising ride up a mountain in the Philippines

20

DO YOU EVER GET SICK?

"Do you ever get sick on the trips you take? Aren't you afraid you'll catch some deadly disease?"

The answers to those questions are yes and no. Yes, we get sick. But so far, we have managed to hit the low bar of success on every trip – we bring home the same number of people we went with. But we're not afraid. We take the necessary precautions beforehand by getting suggested and required immunizations, and we're careful when in another country. We keep our hands as clean as possible, use hand sanitizer and antibacterial wipes when away from running water, and wash with antibacterial soap when running water is available. We try to keep our hands off our faces. And we never eat any food that hasn't been prepared specifically for us (no street food). Even with all that, sometimes we get sick - just like we do in the U.S.

"Where you lead me, I will follow. What you feed me, I will swallow." That should be the go-to expression of every mission team member. And, for the most part, it has been the expression of our team members. We've experienced some different foods but nothing so weird or exotic that no one could eat it. Yes, that means we sometimes eat things we don't particularly like, but when you're in a country surrounded by people who have no idea where their next meal is coming from, you learn to appreciate the food that's put in front of you. Sometimes this leads to some digestive issues among the team members.

Most of us could tell you about times when we've gotten sick from something we ate and not always something weird. The worst case of sickness I ever had on a trip was after eating in a Denny's in Honduras. I will spare you the gory details, but it was twenty-four hours of complete agony that forced me to stay uncomfortably close to the toilet in our hotel room. I was advised by those caring for me that I should go to the hospital and get an IV, but I was stubborn. I didn't want to go because our flight home was the next day and I was afraid they wouldn't let me leave. I contacted my sweet friend Pam and asked for help. Her instructions saved the day, and I was able to get home the next day, but only because my sweet teammate, Jamie Dennett, helped me to get there – carrying my bags and making sure I had what I needed. That kind of thing can happen anywhere, though. Probably everyone who reads this could tell of a time when they ate something bad and then paid the price for it later – even in the U.S.

We ask our potential team members to answer some medical questions on their applications because, once we leave the U.S., those team members become the responsibility of the team leader(s), and we need to know what kind of potential issues we might have to deal with concerning a team member's health. We also must take into consideration how much of an imposition it can be on our hosts when someone gets very sick, putting a lot of responsibility on their shoulders.

Only once have we run into a serious problem when a team member failed to disclose their medical issues and was approved to join the team. It was on a trip to Haiti, and this team member, "Bob" (not his real name), had been among the first twelve people from Maine who went to work with Pastor Noël. This first trip of his had been twenty-five years prior to the trip he took with us, and he had never been back to Haiti in all that time. Bob was in his seventies by this time and just wanted to make one more trip before he was unable to do it. Had we known about his medical issues, we probably would not have approved him for the team. We believe he knew that would be our response, so he did not disclose the information when he filled out his application. He just wanted to go one more time. By the time we found out, it was too late. We were already in Haiti.

In some ways, I'm glad we didn't know because Bob truly was a joy to have on the team. His outgoing, energetic personality was enjoyable, and he kept us laughing. But he should not have been there. It made me very nervous as a team leader - as it should have - because he became *very* ill to the point where we wondered if he might not make it through the night. I tried calling the emergency contact number he gave us but never got an answer. There was no way we could take him anywhere, and there were no medical facilities nearby that could handle all his issues. He was delirious – both from fever and because he couldn't keep any of his medications down – and coughing so hard I literally thought he was going to cough up a lung. Marie and our faithful Haitian cook, Rosianie, who is also a midwife, took over his care. They gave him an alcohol sponge bath, ran a fan for him, and tried to get tiny sips of water into him. They watched over him most of the night. I was afraid to go to sleep because I was afraid he would be dead when I woke up, and I had no idea what we would do then. But God was gracious and merciful, and Marie and Rosianie were like angels, and he was alive in the morning and much improved.

There was also another team member who came to Haiti with us on a different trip. He also had a medical issue which he did not disclose, but not because he purposely chose to leave it out. He simply hadn't had an issue with this particular health problem in many years. It never occurred to him he might have the issue pop up again on a trip to Haiti. But if we've learned anything about foreign travel – especially to a place like Haiti – if there's even the slightest potential for a problem to occur, it's probably going to occur.

This very kind, very helpful gentleman (I'll call him John) had an excellent attitude and was willing to do whatever the team needed him to do. He was a great asset to our team. However, Marie came to me one morning to tell me John had gone outside during the night and was sleeping on the ground in the courtyard behind the mission house. Marie discovered him out there and was very nervous about having him outside alone. There were a couple of young men who helped around the house so she asked one of them to sleep out there next to John. He had a machete next to him, too, in case anyone jumped over the wall and tried to cause trouble. She also left the back door unlocked in case they needed to come inside. But then she couldn't sleep because she was afraid to leave the door unlocked as that put all of us in an unsecured situation. So, she asked me what we should do.

I talked with John and asked him why he wanted to sleep outside. He confessed that he had a serious issue with claustrophobia and anxiety attacks in the past. It had been at least twenty-five years since he had any issues with it, so he never even thought about it when he applied for the trip. His anxiety would get so bad he had been known to rip out an entire window – sash and all – to get out of a room at night. And the claustrophobia and anxiety had attacked him again in Haiti. He simply could not sleep inside the house. We tried various alternative solutions for him that would allow him to sleep in a more open area without having to leave the house unlocked, but nothing worked. Sadly, he had to make the decision to go home early because he simply could not stay inside the house at night.

Marilee led a team to Haiti one time, and about a week after they had been back in the U.S., she woke up in the night very itchy. She went into the bathroom, saw herself in the mirror, and screamed inside her head. She was all splotchy and looked unrecognizable. Her legs looked like she had red knee socks on. The rash hurt terribly and felt like it was burned.

It was roughly 3:00 in the morning. There had been an outbreak of the Zika virus in the southern U.S. during that time, so she googled "Zika". The photos of the Zika rash she found on the internet looked just like what she had on her body. She took photos of herself and sent them via text to her doctor, who is also a family friend, saying she thought she had Zika.

That morning she had to go to the hospital to get blood drawn, and they had all the infectious protocols in place. She ached and itched terribly for about a week after and experienced intense pain. She was taking huge doses of

Benadryl for the itch but it didn't really help. Then all the symptoms simply went away.

Confirmation came from the CDC after she was finished with the virus. She was the second case of the Zika virus in Maine. Since it was the month of March and she was in Maine, there was no threat of mosquitoes spreading it from her to someone else, which was something to be thankful for. But it also meant the only way she could have contracted Zika was in Haiti – where the mosquitos were plentiful.

On our first trip to India, I started to experience some weird, random symptoms that didn't seem to have any connection to one another. They were more annoying than anything else, so I chose to simply ignore them. However, on that overnight trip on the train I spoke about in previous chapters, during the second night on the train when we were returning from the Anamani Home, I developed the worst headache I had ever had. It literally felt like someone was sawing my skull in half along the part in my hair. I just assumed it was because of the travel – two nights in a row on an Indian train with very little sleep – and wasn't worried about anything else. I just wanted the headache to stop.

When we finally got off the train, we went to our hotel room and tried to sleep. I dozed on and off but began to realize I had a fever, and it just kept getting worse. Then the digestive issues started. Again, I'll spare you those details, but I was thankful there was a basin next to the toilet in the bathroom. The headache was intense. I could not get out of bed other than to visit the bathroom. All my joints were aching. I. Was. Sick. That lasted for a day or two, and then I improved enough to be able to get out of bed, but I was pretty weak, so we didn't do much.

I was thankful when we were able to fly home, and my condition continued to improve. However, there was one issue that did not improve. My joints ached worse than I had ever experienced before. Climbing up the stairs in my house was agony so I would sit on the steps and just hoist myself up from step to step on my bottom. My knees, ankles, my elbows, and wrists hurt as though I had arthritis. This pain lasted for at least a month or more after I recovered from all the other symptoms.

I still had no idea why any of that had happened, but I decided to just live with it and get through it the best I could. I busied myself doing the work we needed to do when starting a new program, including reviewing the information we had received from Pastor Michael. One of the questions we ask when we visit a new country is about the common illnesses in the area. We ask because it's good for us to know what kinds of health issues the children and their parents might face. Pastor Michael had told us about a mosquito-borne illness called chikungunya, which I had never heard of before. I assumed it was probably a disease we knew by another name, like malaria or something. I had him write down the name and decided to look it up when we got home and then forgot about it – until I was reviewing my notes.

I Googled "chikungunya" and was shocked when the results popped up, listing the symptoms and the timeline of when they appear. It was like checking off a checklist of my own symptoms, including the timing of when they appeared. The clincher was the long-term joint pain that lingers after the other symptoms resolve. There it was - the answer to what was wrong with me. I didn't bother to seek medical attention for two reasons. First, living in rural Maine, I was not likely to find anyone who could test me for chikungunya. Second, the treatment for chikungunya is ibuprofen and rest – exactly what I had already been doing. So I continued my self-treatment, and eventually, even the joint pain resolved.

Do I know for an absolute fact I had chikungunya? No, but the evidence suggests I did. The good thing is if I truly did have it, I will never get it again. It's a one-and-done illness for which I am thankful because I never want to go through that again. But I would if I had to.

Our obedience should never be conditional. I've found when we try to tell God we'll do anything *but* a certain thing, it's that *certain thing* He's going to ask us to do.

We could all come up with a thousand excuses for not obeying the call. I have developed an allergy to every malaria medication known to man, and yet God has called me to visit many malaria-risk countries. Do I worry about it? No. Because as I said earlier, God knows when and how I will come to the end of my life; He already has a plan for it. If He has malaria planned for me, so be it. And the truth is this – I would be putting myself at much greater risk by *not* obeying God's call than by obeying it, even in the face of roadside bombs in the Congo or contracting malaria. Because being outside of God's will for our lives is the riskiest place we could ever be – riskier than bombs or Zika or malaria.

Does that mean Bob and John also did the right thing in going on the trips with us? Perhaps. That's not for me to say; only God can answer that question. But I am confident that if God had called them to go, they needed to be on those teams. We may never know why this side of Glory, but God's purposes will always prevail.

"Therefore we do not lose heart. Though outwardly we are wasting away, yet inwardly we are being renewed day by day. For our light and momentary troubles are achieving for us an eternal glory that far outweighs them all." (2 Corinthians 4:16-17 NIV)

Luke and Pam Brochu sharing a meal with us at our favorite coffee shop in Kisoro, Uganda

21

GOING TO THE BATHROOM

"What do you do when you need to go to the bathroom?? Do they even have bathrooms in the countries you visit??"

I get asked this question more than you could imagine. Most of the time, the answer to it is pretty straight-forward. There are bathrooms in other countries, and many of them are just like bathrooms in the U.S. When a traditional bathroom isn't available, we make do - just like we would if we were traveling in a remote area in the U.S. Sometimes this leads to some interesting situations, as you could imagine, especially for a woman. But none as noteworthy or as great of an illustration about how God wants us to pray about all our needs, even the simple ones, as the time I needed a bathroom while traveling down a road in Haiti. (Yes, a lot of my stories revolve around bathrooms, don't they?)

I love mango - especially a Haitian Baptiste mango. They are one of the best varieties of mango in Haiti. They're smooth, not at all stringy, and have a delicious, juicy, sweet taste. When our hostess put out a large plate of cut-up mango on the breakfast table, I had some. And then some more. And then, when no one else wanted to clean up the mango plate, I ate the rest.

As I said, I love mango. However, there's just one problem with mango. When you eat too much, it doesn't like to stay with you for very long. I had made the mistake of eating a bit too much mango on a day when we would be going out of Terrier Rouge to a community we had never visited before. I had no idea how long it would take to get there and we had to ride in the back of an open pickup truck over very bumpy dirt roads. I'm sure you can imagine where I'm going with this.

Before too long, that feeling came over me – the one that lets you know the mango doesn't want to stick with you for much longer. I was very uncomfortable and started looking around to see if I could find a place to hide behind a bush or something and do what I needed to do. But the road was a narrow one with cactus hedges on both sides, so sneaking off to hide behind a bush just wasn't going to happen. So I tried to ignore the feeling and had a little bit of success.

Before too long, the feeling was back, even stronger. I was fidgeting in my seat, still looking for a place to sneak away and do what needed to be done, but the cactus hedges only ended when we were in small towns with no public facilities. We kept bumping along in the back of that truck, the sun beating down on us and clouds of dust covering everything in the back of the truck, including us.

There were a number of us on that team, so I was not alone in the truck, but I didn't want to tell anyone about the agony I was going through because it was too embarrassing. So I did what I should have done in the first place; I started praying. I was asking God to either provide me a place where I could do what I needed to do or to make the feeling in my gut go away. The feeling subsided, so I began to believe that was how He would answer my request. Then the feeling came back with a vengeance. I finally realized I had to do something more. I had reached the point where it was going to happen, and the only choice I had was *where* it would happen.

As I sat there with my head hanging, going through my own private agony and turmoil, it reached a point where I could wait no longer. If I had to get out and do my business right there in the road beside the truck, I would do it and just ask everyone to turn the other way. Without looking around to see where we were, I simply looked up directly at Philip, and with urgency in my voice I said, "*Stop the truck!*"

To his credit, Philip realized something urgent was going on, and instead of taking his time to react (as is common for him), he immediately started banging on the cab of the truck and told the driver to stop. I hadn't even bothered to look around because it didn't matter where we were. I was going to get out of that truck and get rid of the agony inside me no matter where I had to do it.

When the truck stopped, I looked around to see where I should go, and I couldn't believe my eyes. There – right beside the road – was a small concrete block structure that looked exactly like a latrine! Hallelujah! A latrine right where we stopped! I jumped out and another lady, named Rosita, came with me because she felt the call of nature as well. We ran over to the little building we thought was a latrine and looked inside.

When we looked in, we discovered it was the size and shape of a latrine but had a solid concrete floor with no opening in it. The only thing inside that little structure was a white enamel pot right in the middle of the floor and nothing else. Being the child of a naval officer, I had learned the old Navy adage "Any port in a storm!" at a very young age. So I did what needed to be done right there in that enamel pot. Rosita stood in the doorway with her skirt spread wide so no one could see us since there was no actual door on the building, and we were in a small town.

Once I was thoroughly relieved, Rosita and I switched places. She did her thing, then we went back to the truck, and the team continued on our way. To this day, I have no idea what that little building was or why it was right there beside the road where we stopped other than to say God put it there in preparation for the day when I would be desperately praying for it. I have no idea what that little pot was for, but we have joked perhaps the building was a voodoo shrine of some sort. If it was, I left my offering there in that pot.

Another time we were up in the little village of Ouvray in Haiti, and I needed a bathroom. At that time, they were still working on their church building. It was on a piece of property belonging to a deacon in the church, where the deacon's home was also located. There was no proper bathroom or even a latrine at the time, but they had a little hole in the ground over in the bushes on the other side of the property, which the family used as their latrine for the household. They had put sticks into the ground all around the hole like little poles and then wove smaller sticks in and out of those poles to fashion a fence of sorts. The whole thing was probably only two feet high and only slightly larger in diameter than the hole in the ground with lots of gaps in the weaving. Needless to say, it didn't offer much privacy. Since it was on the other side of the property, I figured I could probably just slip away without anyone noticing where I was going and do my business without anyone paying any attention.

I nonchalantly started to work my way over in that direction, and as I got closer, I started to walk a bit faster since the need was becoming a bit more urgent. Just then, I heard someone shouting my name. I couldn't believe it. I thought I was going to get away with using the latrine without anyone noticing, but now someone was shouting my name. I looked around only to see the deacon's wife running in my direction from the other side of the property carrying a roll of toilet paper up high over her head with the loose end of the roll streaming behind her. It was really a very sweet gesture which I should have appreciated, but all I could think about was the fact that my plan to do my business in secrecy had just gone out the window with a flying roll of toilet paper – especially when a group of kids came running along behind her. And I will leave the rest of that story to your imagination!

Then there was the time we made our first visit to East Africa and met Pastor Bamo. We were traveling in the car in a remote area in Uganda when nature called. I really needed a bathroom, but I had no idea how much further we needed to go. Also, since it was our first visit to Africa, I was embarrassed to tell Bamo I needed to pee. But I sure did. As I looked out the window of the car at the twisting road going up into the mountains with a steep slope on the side of the road, the idea of getting out and doing my thing in the bushes on the side of the road didn't seem like such a good idea. I tried to wait it out but soon reached the point I mentioned previously; it was *going* to happen, and my only choice at that point was *where* it would happen.

I finally spoke up and asked the driver to stop, while Bamo apologized profusely for the fact that there were no facilities I could use in the area. I got out, walked back a bit in the direction we had just come from, and then cautiously left the road and started down the steep embankment where I could hide behind a bush. As I found my spot and proceeded to do what I had gone there to do, I had this mental image of myself slipping and rolling down that steep bank to my death. I pictured the headline in the newspaper: "American Missionary Woman Dies Peeing on the Side of the Road in Uganda," and I could only laugh.

Another time we were in Guatemala in a remote community. The road out to the community is rough, and there are four rivers you have to drive through to get there. We spent the day in the community helping with a construction project and then packed up to head back to the mission house. As we were making our way back down the rough road to get out to the main highway, the skies opened, and the rain poured down in buckets. When we came to the last and biggest river, the water had risen to the point where it was not safe to drive through. We had no option but to sit there and wait for the storm to pass and the water level to drop back down to normal.

It took quite some time for that to happen, and, of course, even though I had used the bathroom before getting into the truck to leave, I had to go again. Thankfully there was a lot of vegetation beside the road, which was rather like a jungle. I knew I could find a spot in there to do what needed to be done without being seen. I told Pastor Merari I needed to get out of the vehicle and hide behind a bush, but I made the mistake of asking if there were any snakes in the area. He replied saying, "Only little ones – like nine meters." Merari likes to tease, but at that moment, I really didn't know if I should believe him or not.

Reaching the "only choice is *where* it will happen" point

again, I got out, braved the rain, and wove my way into the jungle-y area beside the road. I was very well hidden from view with all the vegetation and felt comfortable doing my business there, knowing no one could possibly see me. While I was doing what I went there to do, I had this image in my head of a huge python slithering down one of the trees right beside me, hidden from view by all the vines, and imagined another newspaper headline. And I could only laugh.

As weird as this may sound, bodily functions are one of the things that unite us. Everyone, everywhere, has to respond to the call of nature. It's just a part of life whether you're American, Ugandan, Haitian, or Guatemalan. It's something we all have in common, and it's something we can all understand. So I've learned not to be embarrassed now when I have to tell someone I need to respond to that call. Because, chances are, they've been in that same spot themselves – needing to go but not knowing where to do it and being embarrassed to ask. It's simply something that's common to all of us as humans. So what's the answer to that initial question about what I do when I need to go to the bathroom? It's simple – I find a place and go.

"Do not be anxious about anything, but in every situation, by prayer and petition, with thanksgiving, present your requests to God." (Philippians 4:6 NIV)

Marilee preparing to attempt using a "squatty potty" in Myanmar

22

PROFOUNDLY CHANGED

"How many people have you taken on trips with your ministry? Has making a trip had any kind of long-term impact on anyone?"

The primary purpose of our trips may be gathering information on the children and adults in the program and strengthening our relationships with our partners. But we can't overlook the impact participation in one of our trips may have on an individual team member. Our dear friend and team leader of our first trip to Haiti, Allan Stanford, likes to say, "If I were king, everyone would have to go once." We realize it is not possible for everyone to make a trip like this, but we do agree with Allan's sentiment and encourage people to step out in faith and make a trip.

Over the years, His Hands has taken close to two hundred different people on our mission trips. For some, it's been a one-and-done experience. They go home with their photos, put them in an album, put it up on the shelf, and that's the end of it. It can be difficult for us to understand how that can happen when the experience has the potential to be life-changing. Others may go on a few trips with us, become a sponsor, and then life gets in the way, and we lose touch with them. There are others who are all in: they make multiple trips, sponsor children, become a volunteer, promote the ministry, the whole works. Even though we don't understand why one person walks away seemingly untouched while others jump into the deep end with us, we have to trust God's plan in the life of each individual. We know His plan is perfect, and He doesn't necessarily intend for everyone who travels with us to become a long-term volunteer. But we love it when He does.

To start with, as you have already seen, I was one of those people who were profoundly changed by going on a mission trip. For me, the end result was so much more than simply going to serve our brothers and sisters in another country. I couldn't foresee that before I went, and it's probably a good thing. I feel certain if God had shown me what He had in store for me beyond that first trip, I probably wouldn't have gone. It would have been too scary and overwhelming. Even though that first trip dramatically changed me, I have continued to be changed by being molded and shaped into a person God can use to accomplish His purposes. I'm not a big fan of change, but I realize now how necessary it is in order to be fit for His service. Even though all that molding and shaping can be very uncomfortable, I wouldn't have it any other way.

My friend Ellen is another one who has been profoundly changed – not so much in how she views the world but in how she views serving in Haiti. On her first trip with us, Ellen struggled with the things she saw and experienced in Haiti. Some of the cultural differences were very difficult for her to accept or overlook. The inescapable heat was difficult for her too. She is a Floridian, but in Florida we have air conditioning, which allows us to escape the blistering heat. We don't have access to that luxury when we're in Haiti, so it's difficult for someone who is accustomed to that option to be able to endure the heat without it. In one of our evening debriefing sessions on the trip, she confessed she was going to have a difficult time being able to find anything positive to share with her small group when she got back home. In light of her confession, I felt confident she would never make another trip with us. But God had other plans. He touched Ellen's heart, and she has been on every single Haiti trip we have made since the first time she went. She has come to love Haiti as a second home and has deep love and affection for our brothers and sisters there.

Melisa only made one trip with us, but the impact her trip to Haiti had on her was powerful. After we returned to the U.S., she sent me an email pouring out her heart concerning how she had been wrecked by that trip. In it, she said, "Ever since Haiti, God is literally *all* I want to talk about, think about, be about! I feel like I suck at functioning as a normal person in this world...I feel an overflowing sense of love and compassion for [people]. And even in [life] situations, an overwhelming satisfaction in trusting in God...*How can something be so powerful, amazing, and life-changing*?? It's so beyond anything I can ever understand. How can something change me so much - literally from the inside out? How could a one-week trip have such an amazing impact on my life and completely alter my chain of thought and my way of living?? But more so, how do I function in the ways of the world when we aren't supposed to be of this world? I've never felt more on track in my life..."

Melisa "gets it" now, and we love it when God allows that to happen.

I met Jessi Culyer on our ministry's first trip to Nicaragua. Jessi was there with another ministry that also serves our Nicaraguan partner. There were actually four different ministries there at the same time, and it was good for all of us to meet and to learn about how each one of those ministries is serving our partner. It was 2018, and we already had several other new opportunities for service on the horizon. With those in mind, our board of directors had instructed us to be praying for God to provide a coordinator for this new program.

While Marilee and I were in Nicaragua, we talked a lot about various people we knew who already had an interest in our ministry, but none of them seemed to be the perfect fit for the new Nicaragua program. As we spent time there and spent time with the people from the other ministries who were there, Jessi began to stick out in my mind. I can't explain why but I felt like God was nudging me to talk to her about becoming a part of His Hands and serving as the Nicaragua program coordinator. I shared this with Marilee, and she had been feeling the same thing. So on our last night in-country, I took Jessi aside and asked her about joining us. She asked for some time to pray about it, but within a few days of our return to the U.S., she and I were on the phone, and she was saying yes.

Then she wrote a post on her blog, which is normally about nutrition and health, sharing how God had wrecked her too on her first mission trip to Nicaragua. Here is just a portion of what she wrote: "I struggle every month as I talk to so many who want to change their health and have all the access in the world and yet do nothing about it because their priorities are elsewhere. Meanwhile, 3,000 miles away, people would love to have this problem and are instead praying just to be able to eat.

"...Busyness is the drug keeping people in hiding and missing out on connection – true, deep, meaningful relationships. When you are stripped of everything, and all of your brokenness laid bare – people taking pictures with their $800 phones, complaining about toilets that don't flush, partial walls, mosquito nets, hard beds, no hot water, fear of parasites, no Über, Clicklist, Amazon Prime, or comfort food – all you have is connection.

"...Whatever you do for the least of these... Everything I take for granted could be given to help a mom take care of her bed-ridden dying child for food, medicine, and transportation to physical therapy, so her child doesn't end up stiff and straight as a board. What have I spent my money on? A smartphone, cable, gym membership, Le Tote, and Blue Apron. You can see God more clearly when all of the distractions are taken away. These people don't have a Plan B, a backup plan. All they have is their faith in God. It's easy to deny God exists when you are living comfortably. You live differently, pray differently or not at all, and treat others differently when you don't have anything else to depend on *But God*.

"...People question if there is a God when they see suffering. People pray away suffering, but it's in the suffering where God meets you. This life is preparing us for how we will spend eternity...Life was never about us, but what we can do for others. It's not about what church we attend, what prayers we pray, or what songs we sing. It is about our heart. The heart of the matter is a matter of the heart. We can't earn our way into eternity by doing the right things.

"...What is the point of all of this? We have all the

things, and it is utterly meaningless. It's all meaningless. How do I reconcile going from people who have nothing to people who have all the things? Maybe that is the point. Human nature is to try and fix things, but this cannot simply be fixed by my own strength. There is no rational, human way to reconcile this. Be careful what you pray for. My longest prayer has been, 'Break my heart for what breaks yours.' Well, it's broken. Now, I wait for what is next. ...Part of my broken heart is in Nicaragua. This is not the end."

We all know the rest of the story now, at least in part. Jessi is the coordinator of our Nicaragua program and is using what God revealed to her on that first trip to motivate her to continue serving His children in Nicaragua.

I can never forget what I heard Matt say to Carlyn when he called her after we arrived back in the U.S. at the end of his first trip to Haiti. "Carlyn, things are going to change." Yes, things did change. Matt became involved with our ministry, served on our board of directors, and made trips to Haiti, bringing Carlyn along at least once. He and Carlyn fell in love with the country and its people. Serving those people and growing in relationships with them had such a powerful impact on Matt and Carlyn they decided to complete their family by adopting their three children from a children's home in Haiti – the same children's home Holly's friend had spoken about in her trip report which motivated Holly's desire to go to Haiti so many years earlier.

We don't always know what God plans to do with the things He allows us to experience. But we do know He has a plan, and everything that happens to us is part of His intricate plan, and it's incredible.

But the most incredible change happened in the life of a

woman named Maureen. She only made one trip with us, coming along with a friend who had traveled with us several times. At the time of that trip, she knew about God but didn't know Him personally. She didn't understand what that meant. She thought people who were *religious* were a little nutty. Then she made a trip with us and saw that we aren't religious. Our faith in Christ is an integral part of who we are and the motivation for why we serve. She listened to us as we shared our hearts with one another during our evening devotions together. She saw our faith lived out not only in our lives but in the lives of our partners, and it made a powerful impression. She carried that impression with her even after she returned to the U.S. Then, she received a devastating diagnosis of terminal cancer. She began to talk with her friend about what she had seen and what she had learned while on the trip with us and in her conversations with her friend after returning home. Her friend continued to share with her about Jesus and supported her through her battle with cancer. Finally, Maureen told her friend, "I want to believe what you believe. I want to believe in Christ." And now she does.

At the time of this writing, Maureen recently stepped into eternity. But now we know she will be spending eternity in Glory, and there is no greater transformation than that.

"Such confidence we have through Christ before God. Not that we are competent in ourselves to claim anything for ourselves, but our competence comes from God. He has made us competent as ministers of a new covenant—not of the letter but of the Spirit; for the letter kills, but the Spirit gives life...And we all, who with unveiled faces contemplate the Lord's glory, are being transformed into his image with ever-increasing glory, which comes from the Lord, who is the Spirit." (1 Corinthians 3:4-6, 18 NIV)

Jessi in Nicaragua with the little girl their family sponsors

23

LOVE IN ANY LANGUAGE

"How can you develop true relationships with people you may only see once, or have several years pass in between the times you see one another, especially when you don't even speak the same language?"

Over the years, we have been blessed to develop many close, meaningful relationships with our partners and with those we serve through our partners. These relationships are only a small taste of what heaven will be like. While it may seem strange or difficult to have a close bond with someone you might not see for years at a time or with whom you might not share a common language, our bonds are all created and strengthened through our common bond in Jesus Christ and our love and care for one another. The differences serve to emphasize the unifying bond we have in Jesus, and these relationships will continue even if the ministry comes to an end one day.

One such bond came about on one of our Haiti trips. We went to visit the home of a friend and discovered her husband was deathly ill. He was curled up in the fetal position on the floor of their living room and had been that way for months. When I asked Marie about it, she told me there was nothing that could be done for him and his death was imminent. He had five young children at the time and his wife, our friend, was pregnant with their sixth child, so it was heartbreaking when he passed away a few days later. We wanted to do something to help, so we left some money with Pastor Noël to help pay for the funeral expenses, as these costs can be significant in Haiti. A few months later, Pastor Noël was visiting us in Maine and told me our friend had delivered her baby - a healthy baby girl. As a way to thank us and honor us for helping her with her husband's funeral expenses, she decided to name her baby Bethanie, after our daughter, Bethany, who had been with us when we visited her home that day. There was some concern over Bethanie's health since her father had died of an illness that could have been passed to Bethanie while she was still in the womb. She did struggle for the first couple of years but has since grown into a beautiful, healthy, and happy young lady. It has been a joy and an honor for us to see this Haitian Bethanie overcome a difficult start and thrive, and it's also a joy for us to hear her name and remember where it came from.

On our first trip to the Philippines, Bea and I met a sweet young girl named Penny. She is the daughter of one of the pastors with whom we are partnered. Penny spent most of that first trip with us, going with us from church to church and staying with us at the home of her aunt, who was hosting us. Penny was nine years old at the time and was put into the sponsorship program. When Bea discovered Penny was on the sponsorship list, she very quickly made the decision to sponsor her and continued the sponsorship up until she passed away seven years later. The year after Bea died, I made a return trip to the Philippines with the team and saw Penny again. It was a bittersweet reunion since Penny knew of Bea's passing and knew she had not only lost a sweet friend but had also lost her sponsor. At that moment, God spoke to my heart and told me to pick up where Bea had been forced to leave off and continue Penny's sponsorship on Bea's behalf. I responded to that nudge and picked up the torch for Bea and have continued to support and encourage Penny as she moves up into her university education. She communicates with me from time to time, sharing with me about her life and her dreams. It has been a joy to watch her grow and mature into a lovely young woman who loves God and loves her family. It is an honor to play a very small part in helping her achieve her goals.

Our board member, Lorraine Mitchell, began sponsoring a little four-year-old girl named Staylande in 2003. Then in 2004, Lorraine made her first trip to Haiti with us. When the team went to the school to see the preschool classes, Lorraine was excited to reach the five-year-old class and look for Staylande's little face in the sea faces in the classroom. She didn't have to look far: Staylande was right in the front row! Lorraine knew her the instant she laid eyes on her, and the tears started to flow. She was so excited to meet the little girl she had been praying for and to see her with her own eyes.

Over the years, Lorraine and Staylande have stayed connected. During one team visit, Staylande's mother brought Staylande to the mission house to spend some time with us. We were surprised to discover she had been sent over with pajamas to spend the night! We didn't have an extra bed for her, so Lorraine and Staylande shared a twin bed for the night and neither one minded.

During a health crisis Lorraine experienced, Staylande and her family prayed fervently for her and expressed praise and thanks to God when Lorraine recovered and was able to travel to Haiti again. Lorraine has become a grandmother of sorts to Staylande and has continued to support her – even after Staylande completed secondary school and left the sponsorship program. This year is Staylande's final year in university, and Lorraine has helped her through all four years.

Staylande, who is now twenty-one years old, has expressed her gratitude many times with her expressions of thanks and her outpouring of love for her adopted grandmother, Lorraine. Lorraine has never learned to speak Creole, and Staylande and her family do not speak English, but it has not stood in the way of their love and care for one another.

Our daughter, Carolyn, made many trips to Guatemala with us. She met the young girl we sponsored there, Mishel, and her younger sister, who were both attending the school during the years Carolyn made the trips with us. Once Carolyn finished her high school education, because of the strong bonds she had made during our visits to Guatemala, she made the decision to volunteer at the school we're partnered with and moved there for 8 months. She lived with our primary contact in that ministry and volunteered at the school teaching English and helping out in the kitchen. She developed many strong bonds, not just with Mishel and her family but also with the ladies who worked in the school kitchen. Carolyn also came away from her time in Guatemala with a new skill – speaking Spanish – which has served her well living and working in Florida.

On the ministry's first visit to our existing partner in Kenya, there was a young man who traveled from place to place with the team videotaping their work. His name was Raphael, and he had a heart for widows and children. He often went out into the streets to feed children himself, even though he had very little financial resources to meet even his own needs. He was a big help to the ladies on the team as they walked through the Kenyan bush visiting the widows in their homes. On one of these walks through the bush, he spoke to Marilee and told her he was an orphan and that his only brother had been run over and killed. Marilee told him he needed a Mama, and he agreed. So she told him, "I will be your Mama!"

Raphael took this quite seriously, and they have stayed in contact, messaging back and forth even after Marilee and the team returned to the U.S. She has had many conversations with him and has counseled him in his life decisions just like a mother would. The goal was for him to come to the U.S. and live with Marilee and her husband so he could attend college. They helped him get a passport, but when he applied for a travel visa, it was denied.

When our first team went to visit Tanzania a year after Marilee and Raphael first met, Raphael took a bus from Kenya into Tanzania to see Marilee, who was on the team. He also became a part of the team as they all worked together with the children in Tanzania. Hopefully, one day Marilee's goal of bringing Raphael to the U.S. for further education can be realized.

When Wanda went to Honduras the first time, the team went to one of the churches where several young ladies were performing some dances for them. Directly in front of Wanda was a girl named Lilian, with a big beautiful smile. Wanda tried not to keep looking at her during the dances because she didn't want to make her feel uncomfortable, even though her eyes were constantly drawn to the girl's face. During the morning, as the team was working, Wanda would look up and Lilian would either be looking at her or would turn to look at her. They just kept connecting, and Wanda observed Lilian had a sweetness about her. She just felt drawn to Lilian. Although she had not gone to Honduras with the intention of sponsoring anyone, she decided to sponsor her and to tell her in person that she would be her sponsor.

When Lilian heard the news that Wanda had chosen to sponsor her, she began to sob with tears of joy – as though she had just won a prize of infinite value. She told the team, "I've been praying for a sponsor. I didn't expect to meet my sponsor in person." When the pastor's wife, Vilma, saw Lilian sobbing, she asked what was wrong. When she heard Wanda had decided to sponsor Lilian, Vilma broke down sobbing as well! She said Lilian had been praying and praying for a sponsor and was growing discouraged, so hearing the news that she had just been chosen was overwhelming. Then Pastor Mario observed all the ladies in tears and asked what was happening. When he heard Lilian's prayers for a sponsor had been answered, he also broke down sobbing and praised God! Such a blessing for the team to be a part of God granting this request for Lilian! It was such a blessing for Wanda to be able to hug her and begin their relationship.

When Wanda returned to Honduras the following year, Lilian invited her to her home to meet her mother. Her father came to the church, and Wanda was able to meet him as well. As a sponsor, Wanda had the option to send monetary gifts and to bring gifts when she traveled to Honduras. She chose to send an extra gift for her birthdays and Christmas. What an honor it was for Wanda to receive pictures of her with a note from time to time! Lilian sent Wanda a construction paper frame she created, which contained a picture of her with her parents when she celebrated her Quinceañera (15th birthday celebration). It has been a joy for Wanda to share in her special moments in life!

Even though Lilian is no longer in the sponsorship program, she and Wanda still keep in touch after several years. It has been a huge blessing to Wanda to watch this young lady grow in her education and relationship with the Lord and humbling to know that a sponsor could make a difference like this in one person's life. Because Lilian was sponsored, she was given opportunities to make wise choices for her future and not be subjected to a life of poverty, crime, drugs, or early marriage, as is so common in Honduras.

On my first trip to Haiti, I met a little four-month-old baby girl named Chama. Her mother was a teacher at the school and knew Pam was a nurse, so she asked Pam to come and see Chama because she was sick. It turned out that Chama was very sick, and Pam wondered if she was going to survive, but she did, thanks to God.

Two years later, in 2004, Chama met our daughter, Kirstin. At that time, Chama was among those children who would shriek and cry when they saw a person with light skin. When it was time to take her sponsorship photo, we absolutely could not get a photo of her. She screamed and hid her face in her mother's shoulder and refused to look at the camera or at us. We had concerns about being able to get a sponsor for her if she wouldn't look at the camera, but Kirstin said she would sponsor her and solved that problem.

Kirstin had worked as a nanny from the time she was

fifteen years old, and she was determined to get Chama past her hysteria over light-skinned people. Kirstin would simply pick her up, screams and all, and carry her around, soothing her with little bounces and soft words. Before too long, Chama was in love. She still would have nothing to do with any other light-skinned people, but Kirstin was an angel to her, and she loved her very much.

Their relationship grew stronger over the years, despite their on-going language barrier, and Chama began to call Kirstin her "white mother." Kirstin married and had her first child; a little boy named Wesley, who Chama called her "little brother." For years Chama would ask about meeting Wesley in person, and Wesley began to ask about meeting his Haitian sister, Chama.

During the time after the Haitian earthquake in 2010, Kirstin was living in the area outside of Washington, DC. She went to the Haitian embassy and volunteered her time helping to pack boxes of relief supplies. Wesley was supposed to go to the park and have a fun outing with his dad while Kirstin was at the embassy. But when they dropped Kirstin off, Wesley got very upset and said he wanted to go into the embassy with his mom. He said, "I want to help Haiti like Mama!" He went with Kirstin and, at two years old, was in the embassy packing boxes of relief supplies with his mom because he knew people like his Haitian sister, Chama, needed help. But they still had not met in person.

In the summer of 2014, when Wesley was six years old, Kirstin and I took him on a mission trip to the Dominican Republic with Jamie Dennett and a friend of Kirstin's. When our work in the Dominican was finished, Kirstin's friend went home while Jamie D, Kirstin, Wesley, and I boarded a bus to Haiti. We decided to take a trip there for the weekend to visit our friends and to give Wesley and Chama an opportunity to finally meet. We did not tell Chama and her family we were coming. Marie Noël knew since she would be hosting us, but she kept it a secret.

Once we were in Haiti, the four of us took a walk over to Chama's house. At that time, their house was tucked back into a neighborhood where you had to walk around a sharp hairpin turn in the road before you came to their house. As we approached the turn, Jamie D, Kirstin, and Wesley stayed back while I went ahead and walked around the corner, calling out to her family. They were shocked and surprised to see me, greeting me with huge smiles, screams, and hugs. After greeting them, I told them I had another surprise for them. Then Kirstin walked around the corner, alone, and the screams, smiles, hugs, and celebration intensified. It had been several years since they had seen her, so they were extremely excited to see her again. After they calmed down a bit, I told them I had another surprise for them. Then Wesley came walking around the corner! The screams, the huge smiles, the shouts of joy, praises to God, and incredible celebration was like nothing I had ever seen before. Chama and her mom grabbed Wesley and held him up in the air like the lion cub in the movie *The Lion King*, relishing in the sight of seeing him in the flesh.

We spent quite some time visiting them at their house that day, just enjoying one another's company and letting Chama and Wesley get to know one another. For the rest of the weekend, twelve-year-old Chama stayed with us wherever we were. She came over to the mission house and stayed with us there, and did everything she could to help take care of her six-year-old "little brother."

When it was time for us to leave, the tears and the grief were overwhelming. Neither child wanted to separate from the other. It was heartbreaking to see them say their good-byes. Marie finally had to distract Chama so we could tear Wesley away from her and make our way back to the bus station. Neither child spoke the other child's language, but love is a language of the heart. They love each other fiercely even though they cannot understand a word the other is saying.

When believers share a common bond in Jesus Christ, things like language barriers, distance, and time are immaterial. Our faith in Christ unites us with a bond stronger than any earthly connection. That bond will survive whatever our earthly lives have in store for us, and one day we will be worshipping together at His throne for eternity. We all look forward to that day!

"Be devoted to one another in love. Honor one another above yourselves. Never be lacking in zeal, but keep your spiritual fervor, serving the Lord. Be joyful in hope, patient in affliction, faithful in prayer. Share with the Lord's people who are in need. Practice hospitality." (Romans 12:10-13 NIV)

"'My prayer is not for them alone. I pray also for those who will believe in me through their message, that all of them may be one, Father, just as you are in me and I am in you. May they also be in us so that the world may believe that you have sent me. I have given them the glory that you gave me, that they may be one as we are one—I in them and you in me—so that they may be brought to complete unity. Then the world will know that you sent me and have loved them even as you have loved me.'" (John 17:20-23 NIV)

Chama and Kirstin in 2004

Chama, Kirstin, Wesley, and Fifi (Chama's mother) in 2014

24

LAZARUS AND PRAYER AROUND THE WORLD

"I can understand how it helps your partners having relationships with people from your ministry. But do you also benefit from those relationships in any way?"

Yes, we have access to resources we can funnel to our partners so they can continue in the good works God has given them to do, which is certainly helpful to them. But they help us in countless ways, not the least of which is by modeling how to live by faith and putting every situation into God's hands. Our relationships are mutually beneficial, and we learned just how much their prayer support means to us when Philip had a major health crisis.

In the fall of 2016, Philip and I made the difficult decision to leave our life in Maine and move to Central Florida to take over the full-time care of my ninety-five-year-old mother, who had dementia. Her caregiver situation had become extremely dangerous, and we knew she would not do well in a nursing home, so we moved to Florida and moved in with her to care for her in her home. We also made the decision to bring Philip's eighty-one-year-old mother with us because she also had dementia and could not continue living alone in Maine. November 2016 found the four of us living together in my mother's home in Central Florida, with Philip and me giving full-time care to both of our mothers.

Then on June 4, 2019, Philip suffered a sudden cardiac death and dropped dead while playing soccer at CRU (formerly Campus Crusade for Christ) in Orlando. He played there regularly with guys who were much younger than him, but he held his own and played well "for an old guy."

It came as a shock to everyone when, without any advance warning, he simply dropped to the ground. The guys he was playing with didn't realize at first that he had suffered a cardiac event. It was ninety-seven degrees that day, and they played at 12:30 in the afternoon – the hottest part of the day – so they initially assumed he had heat stroke. They tried shading him from the sun and poured water on him but finally realized he wasn't breathing. None of them knew how to perform CPR, so they called for help from the security guards on the campus. While they waited for the security guards, all they could do was to shade him from the sun and pray.

By the time the guards called for an ambulance and then made their way to the soccer field with an AED, Philip had been down for ten minutes with no medical intervention. The security guards determined he had no pulse or respiration, so they immediately began CPR. Once he had a shockable cardiac rhythm, they applied the AED, which immediately shocked him. It shocked him again three more times before the ambulance arrived to take him to AdventHealth in Orlando.

One young man was chosen to call me to let me know what had happened, but he didn't mention the cardiac involvement. He simply told me Philip had collapsed playing soccer and was being taken by ambulance to the hospital. I immediately called my friend, Ellen, who took me up to AdventHealth – which we later discovered is the #1 Cardiac Care Facility in Florida.

It was very difficult to get any information from anyone initially, so we spent several hours waiting to see him. We were told he had experienced a heart attack, and they were working on him, including sending him to the cath lab to have a heart catheterization. We went to that area, and eventually, a doctor came to talk with me. He told me Philip had a 100% blockage in his left anterior descending artery – a blockage better known as a "widow maker." They had inserted a stent in the artery, and blood flow was restored but he was still in bad shape and was being sent to the cardiac ICU.

Ellen and I went up to the waiting area for the cardiac ICU and waited...and waited...and waited. At one point, when a nurse came out, I stopped her and asked her what was going on. She went back in to find out, and a few minutes later another nurse came out, obviously stressed and somewhat out of breath. She told me they were still working on him, but his heart was still completely unstable. They were doing their best to get it to a more normal rhythm and maintain it, but, at that point, they had not accomplished the goal. She said as long as they did *not* come out to get me, it meant he was still alive, and they were still working on him – and then she went back into the ICU. I had no idea how to pray at that point. The shock and panic took over while we continued to wait.

After a very long time, the same nurse came out again and got me. She said his heart was still very unstable, but she knew I had been waiting a long time to see him. She said they had decided it would be a good thing to let me have a chance to see him because the outcome was still looking grim. The cardiologist was in there with Philip, and she said I might have to quickly move out of the way if they had to shock him again.

I was completely unprepared for this entire situation. In the thirty-nine years we had been married, Philip had never been to the doctor for anything other than immunizations for travel. He was healthy, in good physical condition, not overweight, and very athletic. He never took any medications for anything; I would have to force him to take ibuprofen if he had persistent pain of any kind. So to see him lying in a hospital bed with wires and tubes everywhere was totally shocking.

Eventually, his heart stabilized enough for the cardiologist to be comfortable leaving. Our youngest daughter, Carolyn, arrived at the hospital to be with me, enabling Ellen to go home. At that point, my entire world came crashing down as reality hit me. Carolyn basically became my mother at that point, helping me figure out what I would need for me to stay at the hospital with Philip. Then she went home to take over the care of our two elderly mothers since they could not be left alone. (A friend had come over to stay with them when I left for the hospital.)

After Carolyn left, I sat there in that darkened room looking at my husband – the man who was never sick and never took any medication – with machines breathing for him and pumping medicines into him to keep him alive - and I broke down. Then I realized what I needed to do. I had been praying and praying, begging God to intervene. But I needed to enlist an army of prayer warriors to bombard heaven with fervent, constant prayer. So I began sending out messages, first to our friends in the U.S. and then to our partners and friends around the world, begging them to pray for Philip. I also asked them to pray for our daughter, Bethany, who had been diagnosed with thyroid cancer just the month before. She was studying to be a physical therapist assistant at the time and was doing her clinical rotations when Philip suffered his heart attack. In spite of all this, she dropped everything and flew to Florida, along with our son, Jake, to be with us.

The doctors decided the best treatment for Philip was therapeutic hypothermia. He was already in a coma, but they had to administer powerful sedatives to deepen the coma and keep him from shivering as they cooled him down. They began cooling down his body to induce hypothermia and allow all his body's systems to rest and to help prevent swelling in his brain. The swelling was a major concern since he had essentially been dead for ten minutes and without oxygen. The whole process of therapeutic hypothermia takes several days because they need to slowly cool the body and then leave it cooled for twenty-four hours before they slowly warm it up again. During that time, they didn't want Philip to have any external stimulation because they wanted his brain to be completely at rest. It was hard to sit there in his room with him, seeing him like that, and not even be able to talk to him or play music for him. Once again, I turned to technology and began communicating with our army of prayer warriors, letting them know how Philip was doing and asking them to continue to beg God for a miracle.

Having partners around the world meant I could always find someone available to communicate with, no matter what time of day it might be. It was a great comfort to me to hear from partners like Pastor Michael in India, telling me not only was he praying for Philip, but he had enlisted their entire church to pray for him. Pastor Roberto in Brazil would often contact me, asking for updates, and shared that their entire church was praying. Our friend Carlos in Cuba would frequently message me asking how "Mr. President" was doing – alluding to Philip's position on our board of directors. It would not be an exaggeration to say there were thousands of people around the world praying for him twenty-four hours a day.

Philip was in a coma for six days. During that time, I learned more about his medical condition, which contributed to the fear I was fighting on the inside. Some of the guys he had been playing soccer with said he was breathing while he was down on the field. When they described how he was breathing, it was determined it was actually agonal breathing – a reflex of the dying brain which is a sign that death is imminent and not actually breathing that can oxygenate the body. I also learned Philip was reported to be posturing when he had arrived in the emergency room. Posturing is a sign of serious brain damage and an indicator that death could be imminent. The doctors were doing everything they could to save his life, but they couldn't make any promises to me. They said they had no idea if he would ever wake up, and, even if he did, they had no idea what kinds of deficits he might have. The cardiologist said, "We can save his heart, but we can't save his brain." At one point, they told me they expected his kidneys to fail. The posturing continued while he was in the coma, so it was clear that not only did his heart suffer a major event, his brain had also suffered a major event, and the outcome was far from certain. All of this contributed to a spirit of fear which would rise up inside me. At times it would be so strong I had to fight to keep from panicking.

Then I had a visit from an angel. The day Philip was

admitted to the hospital, a beautiful woman who was a hospital chaplain came to see me. She had been in the emergency room when Philip was brought in, and she had ministered to the soccer players who accompanied Philip to the hospital. Some of them were quite young, and it was obvious they had suffered a terrible shock, so she prayed with them and comforted them. They had asked her to come and find me and give me the name and contact number of one of the guys who had been playing that day, so I could keep them posted on Philip's condition. She came and found me that night and gave me the info, and promised to come to see me again. But I had forgotten about her until she showed up to visit me a day or two later. She came in and sat next to me, and in her calm, sweet way, she began to share with me about a terrible cardiac event her husband had suffered several years earlier. He was not expected to live but God had granted them a miracle and he not only survived but was healthy and living a normal life. She told me she felt certain God would do the same for Philip, but it was hard for me to hold onto that belief. She was the first person in the hospital who had offered me any hope for a positive outcome.

While she spoke to me, I couldn't help but notice she had an accent. The accent combined with her beautiful dark skin made me wonder about her heritage. I asked her about it, and she told me she was from Haiti. I started to cry then and told her about our ministry in Haiti and how Haiti held a special place in my heart. Then we switched over from speaking to one another in English and began conversing in Creole. It was such a special blessing to me to be able to visit with this sweet Haitian woman, who called herself Chaplain Judy, and speak with her in my second heart language. Before she left, Chaplain Judy asked me if it would be okay if she went over and sang a hymn to Philip in Creole. I told her we would both love that, so she went over and stood by his bedside and began to sing. The joy and the peace that filled my heart as she sang was nothing short of a miracle. The song seemed familiar, but I couldn't place it. I just assumed it was a hymn I had heard in Haiti sometime, but it hardly mattered. Just listening to her sing brought everything out, and I was finally able to sob like I hadn't sobbed before, releasing all that pent-up fear and anxiety. It honestly felt like I had been visited by an angel. She promised me she would be back and promised me Philip would be okay, and then she left.

After Chaplain Judy's visit, I would still experience fear from time to time but nothing like I had before she came. As I reflected on what I was feeling, I was reminded of some scripture I had read recently before Philip's heart attack. It was the story of when God asked Abraham to sacrifice Isaac. I had heard this story all my life and had read it many times before, but when I read it just before Philip's cardiac event, I was hit by something I hadn't really considered before. We all know about Abraham's obedience, even though it didn't make sense to him. We know God provided a ram in place of Isaac. But what I hadn't really considered before was how Abraham simply obeyed. He didn't question God or hesitate to act. He simply did what God asked without asking Him how He was going to work things out. He acted in obedience right up to the point of placing Isaac on the altar and preparing to sacrifice him before God intervened. In remembering that, I realized what I needed to do when the fear would rise up: I needed to place Philip on the altar. From then on, when the fear would start, I would pray and tell God that, more than anything else, I simply wanted Philip back no matter what deficits he might have. I wanted him back, but I was willing to place him on the altar and let God have His way no matter how it turned out. If He took Philip, I would accept it. If He allowed Philip's life to be spared, but the lack of oxygen left him with brain damage, I would accept it. And if He allowed a miracle to occur and gave Philip back to us whole and healthy, I would not only accept it but would give Him all the honor and glory. That's how I got through those six days of silence while Philip was in a coma. I put him on the altar time and time again, and each time, God would provide the peace I needed.

After six days of being in a coma, the doctors decided it was time to wean him off the medications which had kept him in the coma through the therapeutic hypothermia and then wean him off the ventilator to see if he could breathe on his own. The process of doing this is difficult as they turn off the ventilator itself but leave the breathing tube inserted, and the patient has to prove they can breathe on their own for thirty minutes with the tube still in their throat. It's hard for the patient to do this successfully since it can be hard to breathe with the tube in there, and they have to fight panic. I stood right there beside his bed, bent over, making eye contact and breathing right along with him, trying to help him get through those thirty agonizing minutes. He was unable to talk with the tube in there, but his eyes told me he was fighting panic. It also told me he understood what was happening and was able to cooperate despite the panic, which was encouraging, considering the very real potential for brain damage. At least he knew what was happening and could respond to simple commands. And at least he was conscious.

Finally, he passed the test, and they removed the tube. I'm not sure what I expected at that point, but I definitely did not expect what happened next. I've since learned what he experienced is common for someone coming off the types of medications they had been using to keep him in a coma, but I had no idea what was going on, and it was frightening. He was paranoid and delusional to the point of accusing one of the nurses of trying to kill him. He ripped out one of his arterial lines, sending blood everywhere, and was screaming for me to get on the bed with him and hold him so we could go to sleep and wake up, and it would all be a bad dream. The bed was covered with blood and nastiness, but I did what he asked simply to keep him calm. I was far from calm myself, but I couldn't let him see that. I was afraid what we were seeing in him was a result of brain damage, and he would be impaired like this moving forward. Bethany came into the room and helped me to calm him down. I really appreciated her presence, which helped to calm me down, too.

Eventually, the medications wore off enough so he was able to settle down. But he had no memory of anything that had happened. Bethany and I, along with Carolyn, had to explain what had happened and where he was now.

Philip doesn't really like doctors or hospitals, and one of the things I had been concerned about was how he would react when he woke up and saw all the machines he was hooked up to and all the things they had done to him. I was afraid he would be mad at me for allowing them to do everything they had done, especially since we had no medical insurance to pay for it. But I didn't need to worry. As soon as I showed him the folder I had received from the hospital and showed him the hospital's motto – "Extending the healing ministry of Christ" – his eyes lit up, and he said, "I am in the best place for me!"

When our Haitian angel, Chaplain Judy, came back to

see his resurrection for herself and sang the same hymn to him again, he once again realized God had brought him to the best possible place. And our tears flowed. We had a wonderful time of fellowship, sharing with Philip about how Chaplain Judy and I had met and how she had ministered to me when he was in the coma. While we were talking, I couldn't help but notice Philip's nurse, who was from India, listening to our conversation. She had a smile on her face, and suddenly she spoke up. She said, "My soul is stirring listening to your conversation. I see that you are believers. I am a believer too, and I praise God for all He has done here and what He will continue to do." That day was the first and only day she was assigned to be Philip's nurse. Honestly, it was like God had sent another angel to us, and we experienced a time of praise and worship together on an international level.

Over the next few days, as his mind cleared more and more and he was able to fully grasp what had taken place, he would get overcome with emotion and would shout out, "I am in the *best place! I can't die! I've got too many people praying for me!!*" He would cry like a small child, but they were tears of joy, and the words he said were true. There were literally thousands of people around the world who were beseeching God on our behalf, begging Him to return Philip to us. And the miracle is He chose to do exactly that! Philip has returned to us, *fully restored – praise God*!!! He has no mental deficits, even though he was dead for ten minutes on that soccer field, earning him the new nickname of Lazarus.

A short time before Philip's cardiac event, he had watched a video message by Jim Cymbala of the Brooklyn Tabernacle with his men's small group from church. The theme of the message was on prayer and how we should never give up on praying for someone. It really impressed him, and he asked me to listen to it with him a day or two after hearing it at the men's meeting, which we did. After he woke up in the hospital and was able to navigate on his phone without help, he found the video and listened to it again. He had no memory of listening to it previously with his men's group or with me. He was struck again with the power of Jim Cymbala's message and asked me to listen to it with him. I told him he had heard it before, and we had listened to it together already – which shocked him – but I told him I would be happy to listen to it with him again. So, we did. When we reached the end of the message, my tears started to flow again when Jim Cymbala began to sing *the very same hymn* our Haitian angel had sung to us in Creole – only Jim sang it in English, and we could fully grasp the words.

"Pass me not, O gentle Savior
Hear my humble cry
While on others Thou art calling
Do not pass me by
Savior, Savior
Hear my humble cry
While on others Thou art calling
Do not pass me by

Let me at Thy throne of mercy
Find a sweet relief
Kneeling there in deep contrition
Help my unbelief
Savior, Savior
Hear my humble cry
While on others Thou art calling

Do not pass me by

Trusting only in Thy merit
    Would I seek Thy face
    Heal my wounded, broken spirit
    Save me by Thy grace
    Savior, Savior
    Hear my humble cry
    While on others Thou art calling
    Do not pass me by

Thou the spring of all my comfort
    More than life to me
    Whom have I on earth beside Thee?
    Whom in Heav'n but Thee?
    Savior, Savior
    Hear my humble cry
    While on others Thou art calling
    Do not pass me by
    While on others Thou art calling
    Do not pass me by"[1]

God had planted that message in our hearts before we experienced what He had planned for us. He sent a Haitian angel to sing that song for us even when I didn't remember where we had heard it before. I don't ever remember hearing it anywhere else. It's not one we sang in our church when I was younger, and I have no memory of ever hearing it before we heard it at the end of Jim Cymbala's message. Yet, after she sang it for me that first time, I felt such peace. I believe it is because deep down in my spirit, I felt the power of the unrelenting prayers of our friends around the world. They never gave up praying even when it seemed like there was no reason for hope – just as Jim Cymbala had spoken about in his message. There are no coincidences in God's plan, and it's such a blessing when He gives us a glimpse of the front side of the tapestry He is weaving in our lives.

Philip spent a total of fifteen days in AdventHealth, most of which were spent in the ICU, with an untold number of medications, procedures, tests, medical interventions, etc. We tried not to dwell on what it would cost and simply trusted God to provide for this need as well. Before we left the hospital, I spoke with a woman from the finance department and gave her the information she needed about our financial situation. Neither of us was working because our job at the time was giving full-time care to both of our mothers. Our household income consisted of their pensions and the four of us lived on what they had coming in, so it was actually their financial information I gave to the finance department. When the woman looked at the information, she said she was sure we would qualify for assistance. We felt a little better about our situation but still didn't know how we would be able to pay for whatever they would charge us.

We went home not having paid anything for the incredible care Philip received. After he had been home for a few weeks, the bills started to show up in our mailbox. We paid a couple of them, but then the hospital bill arrived, and we were shocked to see the total, which was just a few dollars short of $300,000! The total they were asking us to pay had been adjusted down to around $79,000, but even that amount was beyond what we could manage. Philip decided to call the finance office to figure out some kind of payment plan. He said if we had to spend the rest of our lives paying for it, it was totally worth it.

When he placed the call to the finance office, he spoke to a man named Eric. Eric looked up our account, and his system agreed with the bill we had received. When Philip mentioned our situation and asked about setting up a payment plan, Eric replied that we had to send in some financial information and then they would determine what we needed to do. Philip mentioned I had already turned in our financial information while he was still in the hospital, so Eric put Philip on hold for a minute while he checked on it. He came back a few minutes later, and his demeanor had totally changed. His voice was excited when he said he had found the documentation and that our entire bill had been forgiven! *Forgiven – Praise God!!!*

Our God is a God of miracles! He brought Lazarus out of the tomb, and He brought our "Lazarus" back to us fully restored and without any mental deficits. Then He erased $300,000 in hospital bills. Philip is back to all his previous athletic activities. If you didn't know what had happened to him, you wouldn't be able to tell by looking at him or watching him play pickleball, or tennis, or soccer.

Then in July of that same year, Bethany had her thyroid removed. The doctors discovered that somehow, in the time between her diagnosis and her surgery, her body had completely encased the tumor in cartilage. The blood supply to the tumor had been cut off, and the tumor was dead, leaving no possibility for it to have spread to other parts of her body. I truly believe God chose to give us these outcomes because of His mercy and His grace not only to us but to the thousands of people around the world who prayed for us. To me, this is the ultimate demonstration of the power available to us when His body of believers is walking together in unity and agreeing in prayer, to the praise and glory of His name.

"Now a man named Lazarus was sick. He was from Bethany, the village of Mary and her sister Martha. (This Mary, whose brother Lazarus now lay sick, was the same one who poured perfume on the Lord and wiped his feet with her hair.) So the sisters sent word to Jesus, 'Lord, the one you love is sick.' When he heard this, Jesus said, 'This sickness will not end in death. No, it is for God's glory so that God's Son may be glorified through it.'" (John 11:1-4 NIV)

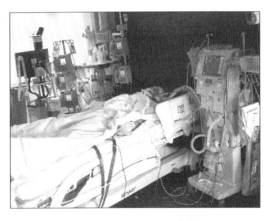

Philip in the cardiac ICU.

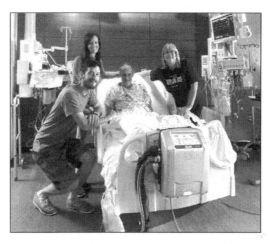

Philip with Jacob, Bethany, and me after his "resurrection"

Philip's first time playing soccer at CRU after his heart attack

25

THE STATS

"How many children and adults do you have in all your programs combined?"

"How many children and adults in your programs are sponsored?"

"In how many locations around the world does His Hands have children and adults enrolled in the sponsorship programs?"

"Why do you have different sponsorship fees in each program? How are those fees determined?"

"How much money does His Hands receive in donations in a year, and what percentage of those donations are used for administrative expenses?"

These are all valid questions, and we are asked these questions frequently. The problem is they are not so easy to answer, especially the questions about sponsorships. As I mentioned previously, sponsorship is very fluid. On any given day, we have new sponsorships start and current sponsorships end. This makes it very difficult to give a specific answer to the question concerning the numbers of children and adults who are sponsored. I will do my best to outline all that information, program by program, but please bear in mind these numbers are likely to change as soon as I finish writing them.

Also, in some programs, more than one sponsor is needed for each child or adult in the program. This is due to the high cost of providing whatever it is that the partner provides to those in the program. Having more than one sponsor covering those costs makes the sponsorship fee more affordable for each sponsor. In most cases, this multiple-sponsor situation occurs in programs where the beneficiaries are living in a children's home or a nursing home, so the sponsorship is providing for both their living expenses and their educational and/or medical expenses.

Brazil – In the Brazil program, we have fifty-three children, all from the same community, who are currently enrolled in the sponsorship program. Of those fifty-three children, ten are currently sponsored.

Cuba – In the Cuba program, we have twenty-six senior citizens, all from the same community, who are currently enrolled in the sponsorship program. Most of them need two sponsors. Of those twenty-six senior citizens, six are currently sponsored but only have one sponsor each.

Dominican Republic – In the Dominican program, we have 454 children from three different communities who are currently enrolled in the sponsorship program. Of those 454 children, seventy-five are currently sponsored.

East Africa – In the East Africa program, we have eighty-seven children from four different communities in three different countries (two communities in Uganda, one community in Rwanda, and one community in the

Democratic Republic of the Congo) who are enrolled in the sponsorship program. Of those eighty-seven children, fifty-eight are currently sponsored.

Eswatini – In the Eswatini program, we have ten children in the children's home and 123 children from three different communities in the feeding stations, which are currently enrolled in the sponsorship program. The children in the children's home each need two sponsors, while the children from the feeding stations just need one sponsor. Of the ten children in the children's home, eight are fully sponsored and one has one sponsor. Of the 123 children from the feeding stations, eleven of them are currently sponsored.

Guatemala – In the Guatemala program, we have twenty-nine children, all from the same community, who are currently enrolled in the sponsorship program. Each child needs two sponsors. Of those twenty-nine children, twenty-six are fully sponsored and two have one sponsor.

Haiti – In the Haiti program, we have 924 children from nineteen communities who are currently enrolled in the sponsorship program. Of those 924 children, 525 are currently sponsored. (Haiti is our largest program.)

Honduras – In the Honduras program, we have 274 children and 118 senior citizens from four communities who are currently enrolled in the sponsorship program. Of those 274 children, 133 are currently sponsored. Of those 118 senior citizens, fifty-one are currently sponsored.

India – In the India program, we have thirty-nine children, four families, and four pastors all from one community base location (the families in the family program and the pastors are spread around in various locations, but the base of the program is in one community). Of the thirty-nine children in the program, twenty-eight are currently sponsored. Of the four families, all of them are currently sponsored. Of the four pastors, three of them are currently sponsored.

Indonesia – In the Indonesia program, we have twenty-seven children, all from the same community, who are currently enrolled in the sponsorship program. Each child needs two sponsors. Of those twenty-seven children, six are fully sponsored and six have one sponsor.

Kenya – In the Kenya program, we have eighty-five children from two communities and thirty-seven widows (from various communities, but the base of the program is in one community) currently enrolled in the sponsorship program. Of those eighty-five children, three are sponsored. Of the thirty-seven widows, four are sponsored.

Liberia – In the Liberia program, we have thirty-five children, all from the same community, who are currently enrolled in the sponsorship program. Each child needs two sponsors. Of those thirty-five children, one is fully sponsored and three have one sponsor.

Mexico – In the Mexico program, we have 120 children from two communities who are currently enrolled in the sponsorship program. Of those 120 children, ninety-eight are currently sponsored.

Myanmar – In the Myanmar program, we have thirty-five children, all from the same community, who are currently enrolled in the sponsorship program. Each child needs two sponsors. Of those thirty-five children, three are fully sponsored and one has one sponsor.

Nicaragua – In the Nicaragua program, we have 171

children from fourteen communities who are currently enrolled in the sponsorship program. Of those 171 children, forty are currently sponsored.

Philippines-Cebu – In the Philippines-Cebu program, we have twenty-one children, all from the same community, who are currently enrolled in the sponsorship program. Each child needs two sponsors. Of those twenty-one children, none are fully sponsored and five have one sponsor.

Philippines-Luzon – In the Philippines-Luzon program, we have 538 children, twenty-three college students, and seventeen pastors from twenty communities who are currently enrolled in the sponsorship program. Of those 538 children, 221 are currently sponsored. Of those twenty-three college students, twelve are currently sponsored. Of those seventeen pastors, one is currently sponsored.

South Africa – In the South Africa program, we have thirty children, all from the same community, who are currently enrolled in the sponsorship program. Of those thirty children, eight are currently sponsored.

Tanzania – In the Tanzania program, we have seventy-nine children, all from the same community, who are currently enrolled in the sponsorship program. Each child needs three sponsors. Of those seventy-nine children, none are fully sponsored, one child has two sponsors, and eight have one sponsor.

In summary, we have a total of 3,363 children, college students, families, senior citizens, widows, and pastors who are enrolled in our sponsorship programs. Out of that total of 3,363 who are enrolled, 1,280 children have at least one sponsor, twelve college students are sponsored, four families are sponsored, sixty-one of the senior citizens and widows have at least one sponsor, and four pastors are sponsored, totaling 1,361 enrollees in our programs who have at least one sponsor – a forty percent sponsorship rate.

His Hands currently has enrollees in our programs in eighty-one different communities in twenty different countries around the world.

Each of our partners determines the sponsorship fee for their program. As I mentioned earlier, we do not take any portion of the sponsorship donations to help defray our administrative expenses. The full amount is sent to each partner, and they use it to cover the cost of the things they provide to each person who is sponsored. What each person receives differs from program to program, and the cost of these things differs from country to country, which is reflected in the varying fees in each program. In some ways, it might be easier to have a set sponsorship fee no matter where the recipient is located, but it would also mean the funds a sponsor gives for their sponsored child might not all go to meet the needs of their child. For this reason, we have chosen to have sponsorship fees that are specific to the needs in each program even though it means the fees are not all the same.

In the last five years, His Hands has had an average of a little over $400,000 pass through our account in a year. On average, only two and a half percent of those funds are used for our administrative expenses – things like office supplies, printing, postage, legal and accounting fees, bank fees, domain registrations, etc. As I have already mentioned, we are run with all-volunteer help and don't own any buildings or vehicles, which enables us to have such a small percentage of the donations we receive go toward what it costs us to operate. All the funds we use for those operating costs come from donations that are either undesignated or are donated for the specific purpose of covering those operating expenses.

While all of these facts and figures and statistics are interesting and something quantifiable we can wrap our heads around, they're not our main focus. This is why it can be difficult sometimes for us to give out these numbers when someone asks. We're not focusing on the quantifiable things but on the things that are difficult to measure. We focus on the children and adults who have been impacted and continue to be impacted by the help they receive. Children like Staylande, who has been in our Haiti program since she was four years old and is now in her senior year of university thanks to the love and support of her faithful, consistent sponsor. Orphans, like Dika in our Indonesia program, now have a loving home environment in their orphanage family and a sponsor who will help to provide the financial support the orphanage needs to care for him and provide him with an education. College students, like Marie Fe in our Philippines-Luzon program, who have been provided with financial support from their sponsor to help with the cost of transportation to their classes and food for them to eat while they study so they can successfully graduate from university prepared to enter the job market and provide for themselves. Families, like Amutha and her two severely mentally disabled children in our India program, are receiving food and financial support to help them survive, thanks to their faithful sponsor. Elderly widows, like ninety-six-year-old Maria in our Honduras program, who lives alone but has a loving sponsor whose support provides her with a monthly care package of food and household supplies. Pastors, like Pastor Joseph Murthy in our India program, who receive financial support from their sponsor so they can focus on ministering to the people in their community.

These are the things we focus on, and it's hard to measure this type of success. Even if we didn't have stories like these to point to or lots of numbers and dollar signs to indicate some measure of success, we would still continue to walk in the good works God has prepared for us as long as He continues to put them on the path in front of us. We have learned we are not responsible for the outcome because God is the only One who can control the outcome. We are not responsible for providing success stories or high numbers to demonstrate the value of our ministry. Our only responsibility is to continue to do the things God has put in front of us and then step back and watch what He does – ***what He accomplishes*** – through us. In the end, this is His ministry, and whatever may be accomplished through it is because of Him - and all the praise, honor, and glory are His. Soli Deo Gloria.

"For whatever things were written before were written for our learning, that we through the patience and comfort of the Scriptures might have hope. Now may the God of patience and comfort grant you to be like-minded toward one another, according to Christ Jesus, that you may with one mind and one mouth glorify the God and Father of our Lord Jesus Christ." (Romans 15:4-6 NKJV)

Steve and Karen Lamb with some children in Haiti

Not The End...

HIS HANDS SUPPORT MINISTRIES

For more information about His Hands Support Ministries
or about any of our country programs,
please visit:
www.hishandssupportministries.org

For information about sponsoring someone in any of our
programs,
please go to the website listed above
and then click on one of the country program links.
On each of the country program sites,
you will find the specific information about sponsoring
someone in that particular program

To contact us or to book a speaking engagement, please send
us an e-mail: media@hishandssupportministries.org

BLOOPERS

Do you ever stay in your seat at the movie theater after the movie is over so you can watch the credits? And then hope to be rewarded with a "bloopers" reel when the credits are done? Well, I've been known to do that and it's always a treat. This last chapter is what I'm calling our "Bloopers Chapter" because it's filled with all those short-but-silly stories we love to rehash whenever we get together. I realize some of you might not see the humor in these situations because I know my sense of humor is strange - a sixty-something-year-old woman who loves finding chickens to photograph in other countries and finds potty humor to be way too amusing. But we feel these little clips are funny, and hopefully, you will too. Enjoy!

What Did You Say?

Several years ago, when our daughter, Kirstin, lived in Virginia, we would drive down from Maine and visit her. On our drive, we always made a point to stop at one particular rest area on the New Jersey Turnpike because most, if not all, of the workers there were Haitian. It was the type of rest area that has several different fast food choices under one roof with a common seating area. I would have fun listening to the Creole conversation around me and would often approach someone and start a conversation in Creole. It was fun to watch their reactions because the last thing they would expect from a light-haired, light-skinned American woman would be hearing Creole come out of her mouth. On one trip, I was sitting at one of the tables in the seating area, listening to three female Haitian workers who were standing near my table having a fairly loud discussion. One of the women was experiencing a common problem for Haitians living in the U.S. Her family back in Haiti was continually calling her and asking for money to pay their children's school fees, buy their books, buy their uniforms, etc. It's difficult for Haitians living in Haiti to comprehend that living in the U.S. and having a job doesn't mean you're wealthy. This woman worked wiping tables in a rest area on the NJ Turnpike and was most likely barely making ends meet. There was no way she could fund the educations of all the children in her family who were still in Haiti. She and the other two women continued to discuss this situation very heatedly, with me sitting just a couple of tables away, understanding every word they said. After a few minutes, they all went back to what they had been doing previously. The woman who was being badgered by her family members was walking around all the tables around mine, wiping them down while loudly muttering to herself about her difficult situation. I tried very hard not to make eye contact because I was afraid she would be angry if she discovered I could understand everything she was saying. Eventually, she moved on to other tables, and I got up and went up to one of the cashiers at one of the fast-food counters, greeted her in Creole, and placed my order. Suddenly, to my left, I heard someone gasp loudly. I turned and looked and saw that same badgered woman, standing by the soda machine, with her eyes bulging out and a look of horror on her face. She cried out, *"You speak Creole!!!"* I smiled gently, and in Creole, I responded, "Yes. You have a big problem with children who need money for school." And we both laughed.

In Honduras, as we were walking around the little town visiting people, I kept seeing these super ugly chickens that had no feathers on their heads and necks. There was one rooster who kept crowing quite loudly. Pastor Gregorio and I kept laughing at this ugly guy who thought he was the most handsome chicken in Honduras, naked neck and all. Pastor Gregorio told me what that type of chicken is called in Spanish - Pescuezo Pelado – and I thought the term was so funny I kept saying it over and over. It made Pastor Gregorio and I laugh so hard it became a "thing." Several years later, when I was riding through the Nicaraguan countryside with our Nicaraguan friends, and I saw one of those chickens in the road, I yelled out, "Pescuezo Pelado!" Our Nicaraguan friends roared with laughter, amused that I would know the name of that type of chicken in Spanish.

We took a team from Fayette Baptist Church to Haiti in July one year. The purpose of the trip was a construction project, which wasn't such a great idea when you consider the fact that Haiti is ridiculously hot in July. Just to torture ourselves, we brought a thermometer with us and put it inside the roof-less church building the team was working in. The thermometer maxed out at over 120° by 10:30 in the morning. You can just imagine how sweaty and dirty the team was at the end of every workday. One evening we were all sitting around the dining room table finishing up dinner. We had not had time to clean ourselves up before eating so we were all a dirty, sweaty mess. Then two visiting Cuban doctors – a husband and wife – appeared in the doorway of the dining room. They were working at a small medical clinic across the street from the mission house and had come to visit our hosts. They were standing in front of a fan and the breeze that was blowing off of them in our direction carried the lovely smell of freshly-washed human with a slight fragrance of cologne or perfume. It was a heavenly scent. Knowing they were from Cuba and assuming they only spoke Spanish, I exclaimed to our team, "Oh...they smell so good, and we smell *so bad*!" The team laughed, but the doctors just stood there smiling with no real reaction on their faces, seeming to confirm my assumption that they did not speak English. A little while later, we were sitting together with them outside when the wife leaned over to me and, in English, quietly said, "I don't think you smell bad."

When we take teams to Haiti, we have to warn the newbie team members about a particular word in Creole. We have the same word in English, but, for us, it's a baby talk word. But in Creole, it's a pretty nasty word. We warn the new team members not to say it because it could offend our Haitian friends. On one trip when we were picked up at the airport, the team split up into several different vehicles and made the drive out to Terrier Rouge separately. When we all arrived at the mission house, Matt (who was making his first visit to Haiti) came to me and asked if I knew the man who had been driving their vehicle. I told him I did know the driver and he was a friend of ours. He expressed concern because the driver had been listening to the radio. Matt said he had no idea what the driver was listening to because the broadcast was not in English, but it sounded like a man yelling with the noise of a huge crowd in the background. He said it sounded like it might be some kind of political rally, except the yelling man kept saying that word – the one I had warned them not to say. I approached the driver and nicely asked him what he had been listening to on the radio. He laughed and said it was a Brazilian soccer game. Suddenly it all made sense. At that time, one of the star players on the Brazilian team was a man named Kaka – the very word I had told the team not to say.

Early on in the ministry, we struggled with finding a good term to use to describe what we do when we see the children in each location. We had been calling it processing the children, but that term bothered me because it reminded me of processing meats or something. We had a very hard time coming up with a better word. While we pondered it, we jokingly referred to the whole thing as "processing hams," reinforcing our desire to find a better word. On one of our Guatemala trips, we had a very large team and there were three different projects going on while we were there. Every evening we would have a team meeting and discuss how the team would be split up the following day so there would be team members participating in each project. I listed off the three things, one of which was processing hams, and then asked the team members to each speak up with their preference. One sweet young guy named Joel raised his hand and said he had a question. He said, "I am willing to do whatever you need me to do. I understand the need to have a servant's heart and do whatever I'm asked to do, and I'm okay with that. I really am. But I have one question. The hams we need to process...are they alive?"

Oh, Yuck!

On another Guatemala trip, we were discussing some of the issues we have when documenting the children. One thing, in particular, was a common problem – making sure the children look as presentable as possible before taking their photos. We place a lot of emphasis on this because we put ourselves in the shoes of the child's parents – if my child was having their picture taken and the picture would be shared with the public, I would want to make sure they looked as presentable as possible. We try to do the same for the children in our sponsorship photos. While discussing this with the Guatemala team, I told them about a very little boy we had recently added to the program in Haiti. Even though we emphasize cleaning up the children before taking their photo, somehow, this little boy had slipped through the cracks, and he had his photo taken with a huge gob of green snot running from his nose down to his upper lip. I didn't discover it until we were back in the U.S., and I was editing their photos. It was so gross I had a hard time looking at the photo to edit it. But it was the only photo we had, so I did the best I could (without having any kind of

Photoshop program to clean him up in the photo) and posted his photo on the website. He was very young, so he was literally the first child listed on the "Children in Need" page – a position that almost guarantees a child will be chosen because they're the first one seen when someone visits that page. But he did not get chosen. Several months later, when we were back in Haiti, even though it wasn't time to update that little boy's info, I asked to see him so I could redo his photo, which we did. When I got home, I replaced his gross photo on the website with the new photo I had just taken, and he was chosen within a few days. As I was telling this story to the Guatemala team, without thinking about how this statement would come out, I told them it was super important to clean up the children before taking their photos because "If they have boogers, no one will pick them."

———

Sticking with the theme of gross things, on one of our East Africa trips, Marilee was interviewing the children. She was sitting at a table in the front of the room next to Pastor Bamo, and beside Bamo was Pastor Joseph, the pastor in that community. Linda and I were working together measuring the children and taking their photos. While we were working, I couldn't help but notice Marilee seemed very uncomfortable and was shifting in her seat with a look of concern on her face. I went over and asked her, quietly, what was wrong, and she said she needed to use the bathroom. Her discomfort was intestinal – something she had eaten was not sitting well with her - making her need for a bathroom even more urgent. As we had never been in this particular building before, I had no idea where the bathroom might be. I told her she would have to ask Bamo where to go. She didn't want to ask him in front of everyone, so she just tried to ignore the feeling and kept working. It soon became obvious she was going to have to break down and ask him because she was approaching that point where "the only choice you have is *where* it's going to happen." She finally leaned over to Bamo and said she needed to go to the bathroom, but Bamo responded by saying, "That will not be possible here." What?!?! Marilee continued to shift uncomfortably in her seat. I told her she was just going to have to go outside and find a bush to hide behind because it was going to happen sooner or later, and I didn't think she'd want it to happen right there, sitting at a table next to Bamo and Joseph, in front of a room full of children and their parents. Finally, she got up and started to go out a door behind the table, but Bamo asked Joseph to get up and go with her. While Joseph was escorting her outside, nature took over before they could exit the building. I will leave the rest of this story to your imagination! (And yes, she is the one who suggested I share this blooper with you!)

Our elderly friend, "Bob," who came to Haiti with us without disclosing his health issues, had a serious issue we discovered the hard way. He had a catheter, and it was either something new for him, and he wasn't used to it, or he had just never learned how to take care of it well. There were constant accidents, but they didn't seem to faze him at all. We assigned Bob the job of escorting the children from the measuring station to the photo station, just to make sure we didn't lose anyone along the way. One day as Jess was passing a little boy over to Bob to take him for his photo, she mentioned to Bob she thought the little guy had just wet his pants. Bob just laughed and responded, quite loudly, *"Well, so did I!"*

On one of our early trips to Guatemala, the hostess at the mission house had given me a list of "dos and don'ts" for staying at the mission house and asked me to read it to the group, which I did. One of the items on that list was "do not flush paper in the toilet." Seemed like a simple, straight-forward request. It's something we're asked to do in many of the countries we visit due to old, sub-standard plumbing and sewer systems. However, several days later, the hostess approached me and said one of the cleaning ladies had told her the young men's bathroom wastebasket had been void of used toilet paper since we arrived. At our evening team meeting, I read that item from the list again and asked the young men if they had been flushing the toilet paper instead of putting it in the wastebasket. Suddenly the light came on in all their faces, and they exclaimed, *"Oh!* That's what that meant!! We couldn't understand why anyone would tell us not to flush paper in the toilet! Why would we crumple up a sheet of paper and throw it in the toilet?!"

Oops!

When crossing the border from Rwanda back into Uganda one time, I needed to use the bathroom at the immigration building. This was a different crossing than the one I wrote about previously, and I had no idea where the bathroom was at this crossing. So I asked someone, and they indicated a particular door in a building adjacent to the immigration building. Philip and I walked over there and paid the agent at the door, so I would be allowed to go in. I opened the door and started to walk in, but I was horrified when I noticed urinals all along the wall beside me and in front of me, most of which were currently in use. I quickly turned to go back out, thinking I had entered the wrong room, but a male attendant inside the bathroom stopped me. He indicated that I was, indeed, in the right place by gesturing towards the opposite wall, which was made up of stalls, most of which did not have doors on them and, again, most of which were currently in use by other men. Still horrified and confused, I again started to turn to leave the room when the attendant gestured to the furthest three stalls that all had doors on them. Apparently, those three stalls are the ladies' bathroom.

Once, while visiting the Philippines, we had a nice recreation day visiting a park in Baguio City with our hostess, Kristine. There were four of us on the team - Marilee and I, along with Janelle and Eva from Australia. While we were enjoying the park, we all felt the call of nature and asked Kristine if there was a restroom in the area. She said yes, and took us to a nearby building. As we entered, she asked us multiple times if we needed to pee. We confirmed that yes, we did indeed need to pee as we approached a table set up in the hallway. It sat sideways, effectively blocking the way so no one could pass by without speaking to the woman there. As Kristine paid her so we could use the facilities, we saw why she had repeatedly asked if we needed to pee. There were two separate restrooms - one on the left for those who needed to do "Number One" and one on the right for those who needed to do "Number Two." Kristine purchased tickets to use the left one and handed them to us, "Ticket for Urination" printed on each. We wondered about the logistics of such a system. What happened if you miscalculated when you had to make your choice of which room to use? The implications were mind-boggling. Once inside the restroom, we saw only two available stalls, so Marilee and I were selected to go first. She entered the first one, and I went into the second. The toilet was set back some distance from the door and sat on a platform about five to six inches high. I stepped onto the platform and then turned to close the door. That's when I noticed that the height of the stall partition was designed for women of average Filipino height. At five feet seven inches tall, my head and shoulders came above the top of the partition - a very strange feeling. As I secured the door, I looked over at Eva and Janelle, who were laughing hysterically at the sight. "You look like a giraffe!!" they guffawed in their lovely Australian accents. As I looked toward Marilee's cubicle to see if she could see me, I suddenly realized that I could see over the top of the partition and into her stall. She was just as amused as Eva and Janelle at the sight of the "giraffe" peering down at her while she was seated on the throne! And thankfully, none of us miscalculated when choosing which room we needed to use.

On our Hurricane Jeanne trip to Haiti, Tiffany was celebrating her first wedding anniversary. She kept going to use the public satellite phone to call her husband, but, as I mentioned in that chapter, there was no signal, so she couldn't get through. As evening approached, she started to get a bit emotional thinking about the fact that it was their anniversary, and her husband probably thought we had been killed in the hurricane. Normally we don't go out of the house after dark (for security reasons), but we asked Marie if there was any way Tiffany could go to the phone to try once more to reach her husband. Marie asked one of the men who helped around the house to go with Tiffany and Kirstin to use the phone. As they started out, they discovered one of the reasons we shouldn't go out after dark – it is *pitch black dark*! At that time, there was no electricity in town so there were no street lights. With the cloud cover from Jeanne, there was no moonlight or starlight either. It was extremely difficult for them to see where they were going. The man who was escorting them had to hold their hands to keep them from losing their way. As they walked, suddenly Tiffany and Kirstin ran right into a semi-solid object – the back end of a donkey!

We often tell our teams we need to try to understand and accept the culture in the countries we visit, saying that if there's any adjusting that needs to be done, *we* are the ones to adjust to *their* culture and not the other way around. On one of our trips to India, Pastor Michael and his wife wanted Wanda and me to have beautiful saris to wear. They went to the trouble of having them custom made for us out of beautiful, coordinating fabrics. They wanted us to wear them to church where we would be expected to sit up on the platform with Pastor Michael in front of the entire church, and each of us would have to get up and speak – while wearing our saris. Now, this might not sound like there would be much of an adjustment to be made on our part, but one has to understand how a sari is worn. Essentially a sari is made up of two separate pieces. One piece is like a short-sleeved crop top that's cut off right under the bust. The other piece is an extremely long piece of fabric that gets wrapped around the waist with some intricate folds that are done by hand each time you put it on, being held in place with safety pins. The excess material is brought up across the body and is draped over the shoulder, so it hangs down the back on one side. Sounds lovely – until you realize the top is essentially a crop top and the other piece is wrapped around your waist with just one section brought up across the front of your upper body. This leaves the majority of your midsection exposed to the world. Being women "of a certain age" whose body types could be described as "fluffy" meant we were exposing a part of our bodies to the world which we normally don't let anyone see. It was with a great deal of awkwardness and blushing that Wanda and I got up there on the platform, wearing beautiful saris that had been custom made for us, showing off our extremely white, fluffy midsections to the world.

Did I Really Just Say That?!

On one of our East Africa trips, we were in the airport in Kigali, preparing to fly home. In that particular airport, you must go through a second security screening before entering your gate. I was carrying our equipment backpack, which contains a metal bathroom scale. It's not uncommon for the security officers to see the scale on their x-ray equipment and ask to see inside the backpack. I'm sure it looks strange on their x-ray screen. So I was not surprised when the backpack came out at the other end of the conveyor belt, and the security officer asked me to open it. He pulled out the scale, held it up while looking at it, and said, "Oh – it's a weighing machine. How does it function?" I told him you had to place it on the floor and then step on it, and the dial would show you what you weighed. He promptly set it down on the floor, looked up at me, and gestured toward me, saying, "Stand on it." I plead temporary insanity at this point because, without thinking, I said, "I'm not going to stand on it! *You* stand on it!" So he did. And all the other security officers took a turn standing on it too!

When we were departing from Guatemala City on one of our Guatemala trips, at the security checkpoint in the airport, security agents confiscated a number of strange, random items from various people on our team. When we got to our gate area, we began to compare notes about what had been taken from us. We had lost things like hotel-sized bars of soap, the kind of plastic marking ribbon used to mark property boundaries (which we used to mark our luggage), exercise equipment, etc. The items seemed completely random, so we were trying to come up with ideas to explain why they had been taken. Lots of the suggestions were silly ones – things like taking items they had seen on a grocery list in their break room. And then insanity hit me again. In the departure gate area in the Guatemala City airport, I shouted out, "No! It's like MacGyver! They're going to use all those things to make a *bomb*!"

Don't Put That In Your Mouth!

On that incredible day when we crossed into the Congo heading to the village through the war zone, as we were still sitting in the immigration building on the Congo side waiting to see if they would allow us to enter the country, Marilee, Donna, and I were sitting there trying to be calm, quiet, and respectful while waiting for the decision to be made. While we were silently sitting there, several immigration officers sitting around the room watching our every move, Marilee reached into her bag and took out a little plastic container of white Tic Tacs, popped it open, shook one out, and popped it into her mouth. As soon as she did, I knew what was coming. Several of the officers jumped up, shocked and horrified that she would take out something that looked like drugs and then pop one in her mouth with them watching! They started demanding to know what she had and what she had just put in her mouth – all in French, which Marilee doesn't speak. I told them, in my broken French, that they were candies and not drugs. But they clearly didn't believe me. I asked her to give me one, which she did, and I popped it into my mouth. Instead of assuring them, this just horrified them even more. I kept insisting they were candies, but I couldn't remember the French word for mint (which is simply *menthe* – duh!) I tried to get them to smell the candies so they could see they were mints, but they recoiled in horror at the thought that I was suggesting they try one of the "drugs." We started breathing through our mouths so they could smell the minty freshness, and finally, the man sitting behind the immigration desk got brave, reached out his hand, and asked for one, which Marilee gave him. Yup. They were just mints. And when we came back to the immigration building again on our way back out of the Congo, he asked her if she had any more.

That first time Philip and I went with Pastor Michael to visit the Anamani Home, as I mentioned previously, they brought us into a room and had us sit on the three folding chairs in the room and then brought us plates of food which we had to eat while holding them on our laps. All the children and adults in the home were standing around the perimeter of the room, watching us try to eat in that awkward position. They had given forks to Philip and me along with tiny little cocktail-sized napkins. The food was good, and Philip noticed it had these tiny little peppers in it that looked like pepperoncini peppers, which he really likes. He stabbed one with his fork and put it in his mouth. Nope. They weren't pepperoncini peppers. They were some kind of super-hot pepper, and instantly Philip's eyes started to water, and his nose started to run. He picked up that tiny cocktail napkin and tried to wipe his nose with it while continuing to balance his plate on his lap and not drop his precious fork. But the napkin instantly turned into a soggy mess, so I handed him mine, which quickly suffered the same fate. All while everyone in the room stood there watching and laughing and trying to find him some more napkins.

On one of our trips to Africa, we took our son Sam with us. He really enjoyed seeing the different sites, including the source of the Nile in Uganda. We did a lot of traveling around, which Sam took in stride even though many of the days were long and tiring. But one thing really fascinated him. On a long, seven-hour bus ride in Uganda, every time we entered a town where the bus would stop, merchants would run up to the side of the bus holding up some type of mystery meat that had been skewered on a long stick and grilled. People who were interested in buying one would simply open up the bus window, and the transaction would take place through the window. The meat literally looked like rat on a stick, but Sam really wanted to buy one and try it. But there was no way we were going to let him eat rat on a stick purchased through the window of a bus, so we never let him buy one. To this day, he still talks about how he really wanted to eat rat on a stick, but we wouldn't let him.

Well, That's Awkward

Speaking of rats, I am petrified of them. Spiders are no problem – you can stomp on them and squish them. But rodents are my kryptonite. One time when we were in Haiti, I was given a top sheet for my twin bed that was probably meant for a king-sized bed. It was draped over the top of my bed – not tucked in – and it was huge. I spent the entire night shaking it out to keep from getting twisted up in the massive amount of fabric. In the morning, as I walked around the bed to make it, I was horrified to find a dead rat on the floor at the foot of my bed. I am very pleased to say I did *not* scream, but I did run out of the room. I have often pondered that rat. What was it doing in my room before it died? Why did it die right there at the foot of my bed? Philip's theory is every time I shook out that huge sheet, I was fanning the rat with the stink from my feet, and he succumbed to the fumes. I guess we'll never really know...

On our first trip to India, Philip and I had an overnight layover in Heathrow in London. We planned to just stay in the airport (remember – we're frugal, so that means not spending money on expensive hotel rooms), so we took our time making our way to the security checkpoint, letting the other passengers go ahead of us. When we got up to security, we were the only people there, so we had no problem putting our hand baggage on the security belt that would take it through the x-ray machine. The only problem with going through security without a crowd is that your chances of being selected for special screening are higher, and that's exactly what happened. They decided they needed to screen Philip's backpack again, so he stepped to the side, and they ran the little cloth over it and then put the cloth into the machine to see if there were any traces of dangerous substances on it. *Ding! Ding! Ding! Ding!* The alarm bell rang, and the red light blinked. So they decided to try the screening again, wiping the backpack down with the little cloth and then putting it in the machine. *Ding! Ding! Ding! Ding!* For reasons we have never figured out, his backpack tested positive for explosives.

They don't think too highly of passengers bound for India, traveling through Heathrow, with a bag that tests positive for explosives, so we were taken aside for more special screening. Our names and passport numbers were recorded, and his bag was thoroughly searched. They found nothing, so they finally sent us on our way. We went into the terminal and found a good place to spend the night. I lay down on a lounger and covered myself up, including my head, with an airline blanket while Philip decided to go for a walk through the terminal. You know that feeling you sometimes get when you just know someone is looking at you? Well, after just a few minutes of lying there on the lounger with my head covered up, I felt like someone was standing over me. I was right. There were two security guards standing over me asking me what I was doing there. I explained we had an overnight layover, so we would just sleep there in the terminal. It was then I learned Heathrow closes at night! Who knew?! They told me they would have to escort me out. I responded, telling them I was willing to go with them, but I needed to wait for my husband, who was walking around the terminal. But I exercised some wisdom when I refrained from telling them he was the guy whose bag had just tested positive for explosives!

———————

On that same trip to Africa with Sam, as we were crossing the border from Rwanda into the Congo, we were standing at the window of the immigration building, being questioned about our reasons for crossing into the Congo. There was a very nice but business-like woman immigration officer questioning us, but she threw me for a loop when she suddenly asked me, "Does he have two meters?" I had absolutely no idea what she was talking about, and I was afraid I would give the wrong answer, and we would be denied entry. She realized I was confused, so she asked me again while pointing at Sam. Then I realized – she was asking me if he was two meters tall! Not because she really needed to know but because Sam is remarkably tall – two meters tall, to be exact.

———————

At that same crossing, when we were crossing back into Rwanda from the Congo, the customs agents made us empty out our large duffle bag where we kept all our dirty clothes in the plastic bags you get from the grocery store. The agents told us plastic bags were banned in Rwanda, so they confiscated the bags and dumped all our dirty laundry out on the floor of the customs building. We explained we had no intention of leaving the bags in Rwanda because we planned to take our dirty clothes back to the U.S. exactly as they were now – in tied-up plastic grocery bags inside a duffle bag. They would not be swayed, and they kept our plastic bags. We picked up all our dirty clothes and shoved them into the duffle bag, and quickly left the building, leaving our plastic grocery bags behind. As we walked out, Sam was musing – out loud – about what had just happened, coming to the conclusion that the plastic bags, which were banned in Rwanda that we planned to take back to the U.S., had just been left there at the border – in Rwanda – where they're banned.

Hello! We're Jamie, Jamie, and Not Jamie

This final blooper is actually a series of bloopers, so it's a bit longer but definitely worth sharing. Marilee and I are both well known for our silliness when we spend any amount of time together. Yes, we can certainly be serious when the situation requires it, but there are times when we find it hard to stop laughing. Sometimes all we have to do is look at each other, and we'll laugh. Our sweet friend, Jamie Dennett, is very different by nature. She enjoys having fun and can enjoy a good laugh, but she is often embarrassed by our antics. So you can imagine how the antics naturally increase when the three of us are together. Jamie D will get serious and try to get us to stop laughing, but that just makes us laugh even harder.

One such event happened right at the beginning of a trip to East Africa the three of us made together – a trip on which we began to introduce ourselves as Jamie, Jamie, and Not Jamie. While waiting to board our first flight at Logan Airport in Boston, Marilee and I started talking about the awkward situation of seeing someone's baby for the first time when the baby is anything but cute. What do you say? My go-to exclamation is, "Oh! It's a baby!" And there are others, but I'll let you come up with your own. Anyway, in the course of the conversation, I told Marilee about how my brother had been born with large ears that stuck straight out from his head. My mother tried taping them back or keeping a hat on him, trying to train his ears to lay flat on his head. Of course, we laughed about it. Then we boarded our overnight flight to Amsterdam and arrived there tired and jet-lagged.

While we were sitting in the departure gate area in Amsterdam, all three of us side by side in one row of chairs, a very tall, somewhat large, very red-headed man came in and sat down in the row of chairs directly across from us. His physical appearance was one that demanded attention simply by virtue of his size and his fiery red hair. And there they were - his ears – extremely large and sticking straight out from his head. I tried not to look at him because I knew what would happen in my over-tired, jet-lagged mind. And I had some success. Then I made the mistake of glancing over at Marilee, who was sitting right next to me. She happened to look at me at the exact same time. And the giggling started. We tried so hard to stop it because we didn't want that poor man to think we were laughing at him (*even though we were!*), but it was impossible. Our sides hurt from trying to hold in the giggles, but we kept trying and looked away from each other. Then Jamie D realized what was happening, and she started whispering, tersely, *"Stop it!"*- which had the complete opposite effect on us.

Later on that same trip, the three of us were having dinner in the home of our partner in Rwanda, Pastor Jean. Pastor Bamo was with us too and we were enjoying a wonderful evening of fellowship around the dining table. Knowing we were Americans, Pastor Jean had purchased several bottles of soda for us to have with our dinner. He also enjoyed his bottle of soda, gulping it down heartily. However, while he and Bamo were talking about matters of ministry, Jean started to belch, quite loudly, as he spoke. The carbonation from his soda was getting the best of him, and the belches just kept coming while he kept right on talking as if nothing was happening. I glanced over at Marilee, and she was glancing at me, and the giggles started. Then Jamie D topped it off by whispering, tersely, *"Stop it!"*

After dinner, I asked Jean where the bathroom was, and he nervously jumped up and said he would take me there. I thought that was strange since we'd known Jean for years, and I thought he would be comfortable just gesturing in the direction of the bathroom. But I was happy to let him escort me there. When we got there, he picked up a few articles of clothing that were in the bathroom before he left me in there by myself. It made me think he was embarrassed because the bathroom wasn't tidy enough for guests. It didn't bother me, though, and I went ahead and did what I needed to do and then joined everyone else back in the living room. We found out later the reason Jean had escorted me to the bathroom. They had seen a very large snake in the house shortly before we arrived, but their attempts at catching it had failed. So the entire time we were at their house that evening, there was a large snake in there somewhere, and they had been keeping an eye out for it without letting us know.

One evening, the three of us enjoyed a lovely dinner with Bamo in the city of Kampala. As we were walking from the restaurant back to our hotel, we had to stop and cross a very busy street. Jamie D, Bamo, and I were all standing in a row on the curb, with Marilee a step or two behind us. Suddenly, there was a gap in the traffic flow, and Bamo signaled for us to cross with him while he continued to talk with someone on his cell phone. Jamie D and I hurried to keep pace with him as he strode across the street, but Marilee was still a couple of steps behind us. Then the traffic started again and was coming at us fairly quickly. It was clear that Marilee's back end was in danger of being clipped by a passing car, so she jumped forward and landed on Bamo's back! He kept right on walking but asked the person on the phone to hold the line for a moment while he untangled himself and helped Marilee to safety. This time it was Jamie D and me who couldn't stop laughing – especially when Bamo insisted on holding Marilee's hand the rest of the way back to the hotel.

On that same trip, when the three of us crossed over into Congo with Bamo, he had reserved a place for us to spend the night at a Catholic convent. It was also a retreat center where people would go on spiritual retreats, so we were welcome to stay there in the very sparse rooms they had for such visitors. We were fine with that, but we were also instructed that we needed to be quiet while walking through the guest quarters and when we were in our rooms since there were other guests staying there who would be praying. We were fine with that too. But when we went into the common dining room to have dinner, we learned we had to remain completely silent while in that room. No talking was allowed in there. It was very strange to be in a large dining room full of people where the only sound in the room was the sound of knives and forks clinking on plates. If we needed something passed to us, like salt or pepper, we had to gesture with our hands since we couldn't open our mouths and ask someone to pass it. You can just imagine how Marilee and I handled that situation...our sides were hurting from trying not to giggle while Jamie D just shot darts at us with her eyes.

And then there was the evening Bamo invited the three of us to have dinner at his home with his lovely wife, Siriaka. That afternoon we had some time to kill before we went over to his house, so he took us to visit some of the shops in downtown Kabale, Uganda. It was interesting seeing the variety of items they had for sale in each shop. Sometimes it was hard to figure out what kind of shop it was since the assortment of items they carried seemed very random. We also couldn't help but notice a cultural difference in the way women's clothing is displayed in Africa. They put large hoops under the skirts on display, hanging them vertically to give the appearance of wide hips inside the skirt, which we thought was a very interesting difference from what we would do in the U.S. While the three of us ladies were in one of the little shops and Bamo waited outside on the sidewalk, we walked around looking at the random items on display. I noticed a pair of teeny tiny thong underpants displayed on a hoop. It looked so funny that I took hold of the hoop and spun it a little bit, asking Marilee if she wanted to buy a pair of underpants. She took one look at those teeny panties on that large hoop and said, "If I put those on, you wouldn't be able to see them." We both started cracking up! And Jamie D told us to *"Stop it!"* And we laughed even harder. When we got back out on the sidewalk, Bamo asked us what had amused us so much in the shop. I told him it was just Marilee and me being silly again. That evening when we were at his house enjoying our time visiting with him and with the lovely Siriaka, Bamo left the room for a few minutes, and we shared with Siriaka the story of the panties on the hoop and how much we had laughed about it. She started laughing and said, "Oh, this is a *fun* group!" (Yes, Siriaka, we are!) Then Bamo walked into the room and said, "I knew that's what you were laughing about!" And we all enjoyed a good laugh together.

"Not Jamie", Jamie, and Jamie with Pastor Jean's wife in Kigali, Rwanda

"A cheerful heart is good medicine..." (Proverbs 17:22a NIV)

ABOUT THE AUTHOR

Philip and Jamie Charles met while attending Barrington College, where Jamie received a B.S. degree in Youth Ministries. Philip is a PK (pastor's kid) as well as an MK (missionary's kid), having spent three years as a child in the city of Lima, Peru. Philip is also a self-employed carpenter but currently spends his time, along with Jamie, giving full-time care to Philip's mother in Florida. They are also the two cracked clay pots God used to begin His Hands Support Ministries. Starting with one partner in Haiti in 2003, God has grown His Hands Support Ministries to serve a multitude of partners in twenty different countries around the world. Philip and Jamie have been married since 1980, are the parents of six children, and currently have ten grandchildren.

(Photo courtesy of David Wardrick)

NOTES

Foreword

1. Songwriters: Tomlin Christopher D / Reeves Jesse Pryor
   Not To Us lyrics © Worshiptogether.com Songs, Sixsteps Music, Vamos Publishing

3. Birth of a Ministry

1. If you're reading this and you're thinking about starting a non-profit organization, please be aware that this $10,000-per-year standard has changed since we started our organization. Now, all non-profit organizations must file a return with the IRS every year, no matter how much money flows through their account. This change was made in 2007 – the same year we received our approval letter and began filing a return with the IRS every year. We found out about the change when the company we used to file for tax-exempt status sent a letter to their clients three years later. The letter said the rules had changed three years prior, and anyone who hadn't been filing a return during those three years was in danger of losing their tax-exempt status. God protected us from finding ourselves in that position without us even knowing about it until three years after we would have been in non-compliance – the exact period of time when the IRS would begin to take action. Bondye konnen! ("God knows")

5. We Go to Africa

1. If you don't know what ululating is or have never heard it, I encourage you to Google that term and listen to the videos that are available. It's amazing!

6. Unity and Guatemala

1. Haitian Ministries - A medical ministry serving the northern region of Haiti, standing with our Haitian brothers and sisters, providing and

developing sustainable healthcare, and proclaiming the Good News. www.haitianministries.us

2. Healing Nations - The Mission of Healing Nations: To glorify God by cultivating spiritual and physical flourishing through cross-cultural ministry. The Vision of Healing Nations: A world that recognizes and declares God's glory as individuals, communities, and nations experience healing through truth and compassion. www.healingnations.net

7. Our Partnerships

1. United With Hope is supporting impoverished and orphaned children in India and Malawi through sponsorship programs and income-generating projects. We believe that every child deserves to have food, access to clean drinking water, shelter, medical care, and education. www.unitedwithhope.jimdofree.com

2. Empowering Action - Combating spiritual and physical poverty in partnership with the local church. www.empoweringaction.org

3. For security reasons, we will not mention Pastor Go's full name or the area in which he is serving.

4. Arms of Love Ministry is a support & resource hub for serving God in Cuba. Our desire is that God would be exalted & magnified through everything we do for His Name's sake! www.facebook.com/Arms-of-Love-Ministry-215165858537257

8. What We Really Do

1. Yes, our partners reported this to the authorities, who stepped in, but the girl did not return to school even though she was welcome to do so.

10. How To Do What We Do

1. In Haiti, any foreigner is referred to as a "blanc," (or "blan" in Haitian Creole) which means "white person", even if they don't have light-colored skin. When we took our dark-skinned son-in-law there, they immediately knew he wasn't a Haitian and called him a blanc too.

14. It's About Showing Up

1. "Pastor Santos" is not his real name. Because he is always in danger of being shut down again, we cannot reveal anything that could be used to identify this dear brother in Christ.

15. Listen To Our Hosts

1. Charles Stanley, "'I'm Going to Obey God': Charles Stanley Steps Down as Senior Pastor of First Baptist Church Atlanta," CBN News, September 15, 2020, https://www1.cbn.com/cbnnews/us/2020/september/im-going-to-obey-god-charles-stanley-steps-down-as-senior-pastor-of-first-baptist-church-atlanta.

16. God Answers Prayer

1. Evans, Tony. 2020. "Faith does not automatically remove fear." Facebook, October 31, 2020. https://www.facebook.com/drtonyevans/posts/3747421931937546.

17. When Things Go Wrong

1. For all you youngsters reading this, the year was 2001. The internet wasn't the "thing" it is today. Google was only three years old and "googling" wasn't even a word yet. At that time, most people did their research in bookstores or libraries, or encyclopedias. (Do you even know what encyclopedias are?)
2. Francis Chan, Crazy Love: Overwhelmed By A Relentless God, Colorado Springs: David C. Cook, 2008

24. Lazarus and Prayer Around the World

1. "Pass Me Not, O Gentle Savior" - a 19th-century American hymn written by Fanny Crosby in 1868 and set to music by William H. Doane in 1870. Copyright – public domain

Made in the USA
Columbia, SC
24 April 2021